THE IRISH AMERICANS

THE IRISH AMERICANS

William D. Griffin

BEAUX ARTS EDITIONS

Senior Editor: Leslie Conron Carola
Copy Editor: Deborah Teipel Zindell
Design: Ken Scaglia
Illustration Editor: Guy Aceto

ISBN 978-1-4351-4996-0

Manufactured in China

10 9 8 7 6 5 4 3 2

ACKNOWLEDGMENTS

I would like to acknowledge the invaluable help of my wife, Julia Ortiz-Griffin, and my son, Michael Griffin. I also wish to thank the staff of Hugh Lauter Levin Associates, Inc., in particular, Leslie Conron Carola, Ken Scaglia, and Deborah Teipel Zindell.

William D. Griffin

Thanks to Georgia Barnhill, Diane Hamilton, John Michael Conron, Molly Leahy from the beautiful magazine *The World of Hibernia,* Patricia Harty, Orla Carey, Deborah Kase, and Deborah Teipel Zindell for their generous assistance researching illustrations.

CONTENTS

For Julia

THE IRISH AMERICANS

INTRODUCTION:
IRELAND AND THE IRISH

Durring the past three hundred years, the immigrant experience has been a necessary choice for growing numbers of Irish men and women. The heritage they bore with them reflected two millennia of life in Ireland. Some awareness of this Irish heritage is necessary to an understanding of the immigrants and their descendants in America.

AN ENVIRONMENT SHAPES A NATION

More than thirty centuries ago, the Celts began their journey westward. Archaeologists, reconciling myths with history, have traced their wanderings from the borderlands of Europe, through Alps and Pyrenees, and into those offshore islands of which Ireland was the most distant. There they paused for a time, gazing out across the great ocean and speculating on what adventures awaited them in the mysterious realm beyond the waves.

These westernmost of the far-ranging Celtic peoples, the Gaels, called their new home by various poetic names, including "Eiriu" or "Eire"—later Teutonized into "Ireland." Others had lived there before them, but it was the Gaels who shaped Ireland and were shaped by it; in Ireland they became the Irish.

(Previous spread) **The Cliffs of Moher, County Clare. One of the most dramatic sights in Ireland, these cliffs drop dramatically three hundred feet into the Atlantic Ocean below. Photograph by Christopher Hill.**

(Opposite) **The swirling mists and powerful clouds of this lush, fertile countryside has been captured beautifully by Christopher Hill.**

Isolated from the Continent, Ireland escaped conquest by the Roman Empire, while trading with—or raiding—its sovereign outposts.

An island ringed by mountains and cliffs, Ireland encouraged its inhabitants to think of themselves as a distinct people. Yet its many rivers and lakes and its stretches of low hills and bogs divided the land into a patchwork of regions and subregions in which strong local affinities competed with broader national identity. Poor in mineral resources and fauna but rich in pasturage, a place of misty skies and rocky promontories, Ireland bred a population of cattle raisers and cattle rustlers whose imagination was stirred alternately by blood feuds and natural beauty.

"Patty's Pat," a rural farm with endless green fields, rocky terrain, and native stone walls is a typical vista in the Irish countryside. Photograph by Kit DeFever.

The Irish social and political system, based upon kinship, kept the country divided among scores of clans, each under its hereditary chief. Their tribal territories gradually coalesced into larger kingdoms—Ulster in the north, Munster in the south, Leinster in the east, and Connacht in the west—but the high kingship of all Ireland remained an elusive prize, held only intermittently.

Shrine of the Stowe Missal, one of the finest examples of the high level
of decorative and ornamental art produced in medieval Ireland.

CLANSMEN AND INVADERS

This drawing by Albrecht Dürer shows Irish warriors, whose clothing, hairstyles, and weaponry changed little from the pre-Christian period to the eve of the Renaissance. National Gallery of Ireland.

This divided nation triumphed over its invaders less by fighting them than by absorbing them and adapting their new ways to suit its own. Thus it was with the introduction of Christianity in the fifth century and the Viking incursions in the ninth. The former brought the riches of Greco-Roman civilization, including the art of writing, while the latter contributed commerce, coinage, and urban institutions.

The divided Irish could not effectively oppose the English incursions that began in the late twelfth century. Instead, they employed a variation of their accustomed flexible response that conceded control of the coastal cities to the invaders while leaving the interior essentially undisturbed. This situation began to change when Tudor monarchs, notably Henry VIII and Elizabeth I, set out to replace England's precarious tenure by forcing the neighboring island into complete integration with the new power structure that emerged in the British Isles during the 1500s. By the beginning of the seventeenth century Gaelic Ireland was fighting for the preservation of its way of life—political, social, economic, and cultural—

against a policy of Anglicization that included submission to the new Anglican state church. Allegiance to Catholicism thus became an essential part of an Irish national resistance to a program of English rule that now included submission to Protestantism.

The 1600s saw the "planting" of Protestant settlers in the northern districts of Ireland—the ancestors of the so-called Ulster Scots or Scotch-Irish. The presence of this new element in the population, alienated from the Catholic Irish, tied by an ambivalent allegiance to the British crown, would further complicate the question of Irish identity for many generations to come.

By 1691, when the Treaty of Limerick brought an end to decades of dynastic war, confiscation, sectarian massacre, and banishment, the moment had come for the modern Irish diaspora to begin.

(Below) **A woman from the Aran Islands. This group of islands off the west coast of Ireland preserves the Gaelic-speaking traditions of bygone centuries.**

(Following spread) **Round Tower at Ardmore. These towers were constructed as refuges for Irish monks seeking to evade the ravages of Viking raiders in the 9th and 10th centuries.**

17

This Crucifixion Plaque, probably from the 8th century, is an example of the high level of artistry achieved by Irish craftsman during the Dark Ages.

CULTURAL TRADITIONS

These Irish who set forth into the wider world were, then, a people chiefly of Gaelic stock, with Scandinavian, French, and British infusions. They were intensely proud of their nationality, but even more deeply attached to the scenes and lore of their particular ancestral strongholds. The ties of kinship and the habit of following a chief were counterbalanced by powerful instincts of self-reliance and independence. Religion was a strong motivating force, though often mixed with sectarian bitterness, yet the superstitions of pagan times lingered in the form of rituals and taboos. Conscious of their nation's artistic achievements in gold-working and manuscript illumination under the patronage of pagan warlords and medieval abbots, the Irish drew more deeply upon their literary traditions. The bards of ancient days and the wandering harpers of more recent time had stimulated a folklore filled with the deeds of warriors and sorcerers, demigods and demons. The popular culture of the Irish, however infiltrated by English influences, preserved a rich texture of songs and sayings, proverbial words and spiritual connotation that embodied the traditions of countless generations. Thus fortified by a deep-seated sense of who they were, and at the same time gifted with a remarkable capacity to adapt to changing circumstances and surroundings, the Irish went forth to face new worlds.

Chi Rho opening page of St. Matthew's Gospel. From the Book of Kells. 8th century.
This ornate page, dominated by the abbreviated Greek form of the name of Christ (Chi Rho),
is often referred to as the high point of the manuscript and the culmination of the style.

A HABIT OF
GOING ABROAD

For most European immigrant groups, the story of their transition to America can be told simply by tracing a line from the old country to the new. The Irish immigrant experience, however, is more complex, for it includes centuries of venturing abroad, a massive exodus to continental Europe in the eighteenth century, and a subsequent diaspora of which the voyage to the United States forms the largest, but by no means the only, component. For all their love of Ireland, the Irish seemed forever to be leaving it.

"A VENTURESOME RACE"

As early as the ninth century, a German chronicler wrote of the Irish as having "a habit of going abroad" firmly established. Indeed, he asserted, it was "almost second nature" with them. This early medieval perception clearly derived from the missionary zeal of Irish monks who were so much in evidence throughout Christendom. Scarcely had the Irish been converted to Christianity than they threw themselves into the work of evangelizing northern Europe, including parts of Britain and Scandinavia, Germany and Switzerland. Ireland became famous as a fountainhead of "saints and scholars" who proclaimed the Gospel and preserved classical learning during the Dark Ages. The Irish, who continued to be highly visible abroad in the later Middle Ages as students, pilgrims, and traders, joined their clerical coun-

(Previous spread) The Battle of Fontenoy. **Anne S.K. Brown Military Collection, Brown University Library. The Battle of Fontenoy, 1745, was a decisive battle in the war of Austrian secession in which Irish troops in the French service defeated their British antagonists. The Irish Brigade led a fierce bayonet charge. This victory has been celebrated by the Irish at home and abroad for more than two centuries.**

(Opposite) Emigrants at Cork (detail). **Style of Nathaniel Grogan. c. 1820. Oil on canvas. Irish emigrants before the Famine were not all in dire straits.**

trymen on the European roads and waterways. During the wars of the Renaissance and Reformation, Irish soldiers of fortune served in ever-increasing numbers, confirming their reputation as "a venturesome race," always ready for wandering and warfare.

The political and religious conflicts of the seventeenth century drove many Irish Catholics abroad to lay the foundation for those schools and regiments that would later become the exile communities of France and Spain. More poignant was the fate of the Irish prisoners whom the English military dictator, Oliver Cromwell, took during his brutal mid-century campaign in Ireland. Several thousand men and women were convicted of treason and sent as slaves to the Caribbean colonies. Irish names, speech patterns, and local traditions in islands like Nevis and Montserrat recall the banished Irish who labored, lived, and died among the African slaves. Not all of the "venturesome" Irish could choose the circumstances or their eventual destination as they left their homeland.

IRISH EXILES IN EIGHTEENTH-CENTURY EUROPE

A stream of Irish immigrants trickled into what is now the United States during the seventeenth century. It was insignificant, however, compared to the flood of refugees that flowed into continental Europe during the same period. The series of political and religious conflicts that precipitated this movement culminated in the Jacobite War of 1688–1691. Following the

(Opposite) **A portrait of Christ from a Gospel page of the 8th-century illuminated manuscript known as the Book of Kells, the most famous product of Irish monastic manuscript illumination from a period when Irish learning and mission-ary activities made the Irish renowned throughout Europe. Trinity College Library, Dublin.**

(Below) Battle of the Boyne. **17th century. Engraving. National Library of Ireland, Dublin. Following the defeat of King James's Catholic army by the Protestant forces of William of Orange, the flight of the "Wild Geese" to continental Europe commenced.**

This "Hedge School" was typical of attempts made in rural Ireland in the era of the Penal Laws to keep the education of youth alive despite an official ban on schooling for Catholics.

defeat of the Catholic monarch, James II, his supporters were deprived of virtually all civil and property rights, and though constituting some 80 percent of the population, became a subject people in their own country. During the greater part of the eighteenth century the so-called Penal Laws that punished them for their loyalties drove thousands of Catholics into exile in France and Spain.

Irish poets of this period spoke of the "Wild Geese" who had flown away overseas, but would return some day to liberate their homeland. Many of the Jacobite exiles did, in fact, enlist in the Irish brigades of their host countries, where they constituted a force pledged to restore the banished Stuart dynasty, and played a role in those nations' wars with Britain. Yet these military exiles were merely the nucleus of a widespread community of Irish settlers. The Irish abroad, who would ultimately be found in many other European lands, from Portugal and Italy to Austria and Poland, included priests and students, sailors and merchants, physicians and craftsmen. Garrison towns and ports, such as Bordeaux and Nantes in France or Seville and Cadiz in Spain, became the centers of flourishing Irish outposts, with their own churches, schools, and even colleges. Over several generations these "exiles of Erin" preserved their use of the Irish language and other cultural traditions and generally married among themselves, with their children being legally identified as "Irish" rather than French or Spanish.

Charles Deas. *Luke Lawless*. Oil on canvas. Missouri Historical Society, St. Louis.
Luke Lawless, a supporter of the 1798 Irish Rebellion and subsequently an officer
in Napoleon's Irish Legions, ended his days as a judge in St. Louis, Missouri.

DON ALEXANDRE O REILLY,
Commandeur de Benfayan dans l'Ordre de Alcantara, Lieutenant Général des Armées de Sa Majesté, Inspecteur Général d'Infanterie, & par Commiffion Gouverneur & Capitaine Général de la Province de la Louifianne.

LE, Procès qui a été fait à caufe du foulévement qu'il y a eu dans cette Colonie , ayant pleinement prouvé la part & l'influence que le Confeil a eû dans fes démarches, appuyant contre fon devoir des Actes de la plus grande Criminalité, quand il auroit dû donner tous fes foins à maintenir le Peuple dans la fidélité & fubordination qui font dûs au Souverain : Par ces raifons , & voulant remédier à l'avenir à d'auffi grands maux; il eft indifpenfable d'abolir ledit Confeil & d'établir à fa place la forme du Gouvernement Politique , & l'Adminiftration de Juftice que prefcrivent nos fages Loix , & par lefquelles tous les États de SA MAJESTÉ , en Amérique fe font toûjours maintenus dans la plus parfaite tranquilité , contentement & fubordination : A CES CAUSES, ufant du pouvoir que le ROI , Nôtre Seigneur (que Dieu garde) a bien voulu Nous confier par fa Patente expédiée à Aranjuez le 16. Avril de cette Année , pour établir dans le Militaire , la Police , l'Adminiftration de Juftice & de fes Finances, la forme du Gouvernement , dépendance & fubordinacion qui convient au bien de fon Service & au bonheur de fes Sujets en cette Colonie ; NOUS ÉRIGEONS en fon Nom Royal , un Confeil de Ville ou Cabildo , Juftice & Régiment dans cette Ville ſavec le nombre de fix Regidores perpétuels , conforme à la Loy feconde Titre X. Livre 5. de la Recopilation des Indes , parmi lefquels feront partagés les charges d'Alférez Royal , Alcade Mayor Provincial, Alguazil Mayor, Dépofitaire Général , & Receveur de Penas de Camara, ou

Amendes appliquées au Fifc : ceux-ci éliront le premier Jour de chaque Année , deux Juges qui feront apellés Alcades ordinaires, un Syndic Procureur Général , & un Régiffeur des Rentes & Droits de la Ville , tel que les Loix ont établi pour le bon Gouvernement & Adminiftration de Juftice. Et comme le défaut d'Avocats dans ce Pays , & le peu de connoiffances que ces nouveaux fujets ont des Loix d'Efpagne , pourroit en rendre difficile l'exacte obfervation , & que tous abus feroit très contraires à l'intention de SA MAJESTÉ ; Nous avons cru utile & même néceffaire de former un Extrait ou Réglement tiré des mêmes Loix , qui puiffe fervir d'inftruction & formulaire élémentaire pour l'Adminiftration de la Juftice , & le Gouvernement économique de cette Ville, lequel fe vendra chez l'Imprimeur à un prix raifonnable , en attendant que la connoiffance de la Langue Efpagnolle foit plus introduite & donne à chacun les moyens , par la lecture des mêmes Loix , d'étendre fes connoiffances fur chaque matiere.

EN conféquence, & à la referve du bon plaifir de SA MAJESTÉ ; Nous Ordonnons & Commandons , aux Juftices, Confeil de Ville , Officiers & Habitans de fe conformer ponctuellement à icelui.

ET que le préfent fera Imprimé , lû , publié & affiché par tout ou befoin fera, & envoyé dans tous les Poftes dépendants de SA MAJESTÉ.

DONNÉ en Notre Hôtel , à la Nouvelle Orléans le 21. Décembre 1769.

O Reilly

Proclamation establishing Spanish law in place of French in New Orleans, 1769. Alexander O'Reilly, an Irish-born general in the Spanish service, reformed the administration of Cuba, began the defense works in Puerto Rico, and then went on to serve as governor of Louisiana in the 1760s after its transfer from France to Spain.

Moving across national boundaries in search of new opportunities, they drew upon a network of kinship and contacts, residing by preference among their countrymen as they moved from city to city.

While the vision of a return to Ireland remained strong, many of the Wild Geese rose to prominence in their adopted countries. Generals like Lally in France, O'Reilly in Spain, and Browne in Austria were paralleled by Archbishop Dillon of Langue D'Oc or Foreign Minister Wall in Madrid. The roster of diplomats, state counselors, shipbuilders, wine merchants, and colonial governors included many Irish families throughout the Continent.

Not only did the existence of this far-flung exile community inspire a sense of hope and pride among their oppressed brethren at home, it also gave the Irish a knowledge of the wider world that many other Europeans lacked. There was scarcely a family in Ireland that did not have some relative living abroad, and travelers frequently noted how familiar Irish peasants and fishermen were with the military campaigns and commercial activities of continental Europe, from where they received a regular flow of information.

The fading hope of a Stuart restoration after mid-century, followed by the outbreak of revolution in France in 1789, brought an end to this dimension of the Irish diaspora. Gradual repeal of the Penal Laws by a British government now anxious to ensure the services of Catholics as well as the collapse of the Old Regime in Europe kept most of the Irish at home while shattering the unity of the transplanted Irish throughout Revolutionary Europe. By the end of the Napoleonic Wars in 1815, the Irish on the Continent, cut off from their roots, had begun to merge into the general population whose descendants would think of themselves merely as Frenchmen or Spaniards with unusual surnames. The eighteenth-century continental exiles had, however, left a legacy of enlarged awareness and bold enterprise to the Irish people. Inspired by the readiness of the Wild Geese to pursue their destiny in a foreign land and to seize opportunities wherever found, the Irish who ventured across the Atlantic in the nineteenth century possessed a readiness for the immigrant experience lacking among their peers in other countries. Their resilience and mobility are well symbolized by Luke Lawless, who as a young man fought for Irish freedom in the Rebellion of 1798, eluded captivity to become an officer in Napoleon's Irish Legion, and eventually made his way to the banks of the Mississippi, where he ended his days as a judge in St. Louis presiding over cases that prefigured the coming Civil War.

THE OUTER FRINGES OF THE DIASPORA: LATIN AMERICA AND AUSTRALIA

The Irish presence in eighteenth-century Spain led, inevitably, to an Irish presence in Spanish America. Military commanders and colonial adminis-

Parlamento del Presidente Ambrosio O'Higgins. **Lithograph. Ambroise O'Higgins, Irish-born officer in the Spanish service, served in various colonial governorships and eventually became viceroy of Peru. He was father of Bernardo O'Higgins, the first president of Chile.**

trators often followed the traditional practice of favoring kinsmen or countrymen, creating a nucleus of Irish officers and merchants in many colonies. Alexander O'Reilly, for instance, not only reorganized the governments of Cuba, Puerto Rico, and Louisiana in the 1760s, but left his protégés to carry on the work, such as his cousin, Hugh O'Connor, Governor of the Interior Provinces of Mexico and founder of Tucson, and Thomas O'Daly, who designed the fortifications of San Juan and founded a dynasty in Puerto Rico. Ambrose O'Higgins, Viceroy of Peru, appointed several of his nephews to governorships, and left a son, Bernardo, who would become independent Chile's first president. Spain's last viceroy of New Spain, Juan O'Donoju, is honored by Mexicans for smoothing the transition to freedom in their country. Ramon Power, a naval officer, was Puerto Rico's first representative in the Spanish parliament, a post in which he was succeeded by Demetrio O'Daly. The Powers and the O'Dalys (whose hacienda was named San Patricio) were among numerous official and merchant families in that island, paralleling the O'Farrells in Cuba.

When Venezuela and other colonies struck for independence, Simon Bolivar was able to raise a corps of volunteers in Ireland to participate in the struggle. The names of Daniel O'Leary in New Granada, Roderick O'Connor in Bolivia, and Edward Sandes in Ecuador rank high among the heroes of the 1820s wars of independence. William Brown, from Galway, is revered by Argentinians as the founder of their navy.

Although attempts to establish an Irish settlement in Brazil failed during the 1830s, Argentina proved a more successful destination for immigrants a generation later. Several thousand "venturesome" settlers made their way to the farmlands and pampas during the 1860s, and their descendants remain a distinctive element in the population, with their own newspaper, *The Southern Cross,* maintaining a mixture of articles in English and Spanish, and a roster of prominent figures (including at least one president) to testify to immigrant achievement at the southernmost point of Latin America.

As the British Empire expanded during the nineteenth century, the "venturesome" Irish were found in India and Southeast Asia, South Africa and

Rhodesia, New Zealand and Canada. Nowhere, however, were the Irish more in evidence than in Australia.

The first Irishmen in this remote corner of the world arrived as prisoners, convicted of treason after the Rebellion of 1798. There they soon rebelled again and were once more defeated.

Nineteenth-century Australia continued to see the rebellious side of the Irish nature. Political prisoners were sent to the island outpost of Tasmania throughout the 1840s, and some of them, like John Mitchel and Thomas Francis Meagher, made dramatic escapes across the Pacific to America. Others organized settlers' revolts and workers' uprisings that made "Irish" and "agitation" synonymous for generations. Nor did the immigrants limit themselves to civil disobedience. "Bushrangers" such as Jack Duggan, the "Wild Colonial Boy," and Ned Kelly, whose flamboyant approach to banditry included designing a suit of armor to repel police bullets, became virtual folk heroes, for all the criminality of their deeds.

By the late 1800s, as Australia became a tamer, more family-friendly continent, a growing number of Irishmen and women made their way to those distant shores to begin new lives as farmers, ranchers, sheepherders, and shopkeepers. They had to make their way in spite of ethnic and religious prejudice from colonists of British descent, and conflicts among themselves, including clashes between Ulster Scots and Catholic Irish, as well as rivalries based upon old political differences in Ireland. Nevertheless, the numbers and "respectability" of the Irish grew with the stabilization of Australian society, and by the close of the twentieth century at least one-third of the Australian population can claim Irish descent, and most do so proudly, including leading politicians, businessmen, and intellectuals.

Juan O'Donoju, general of Spanish descent who served as minister of war and subsequently as the last captain-general of New Spain (Mexico). He was instrumental in securing the independence of Mexico.

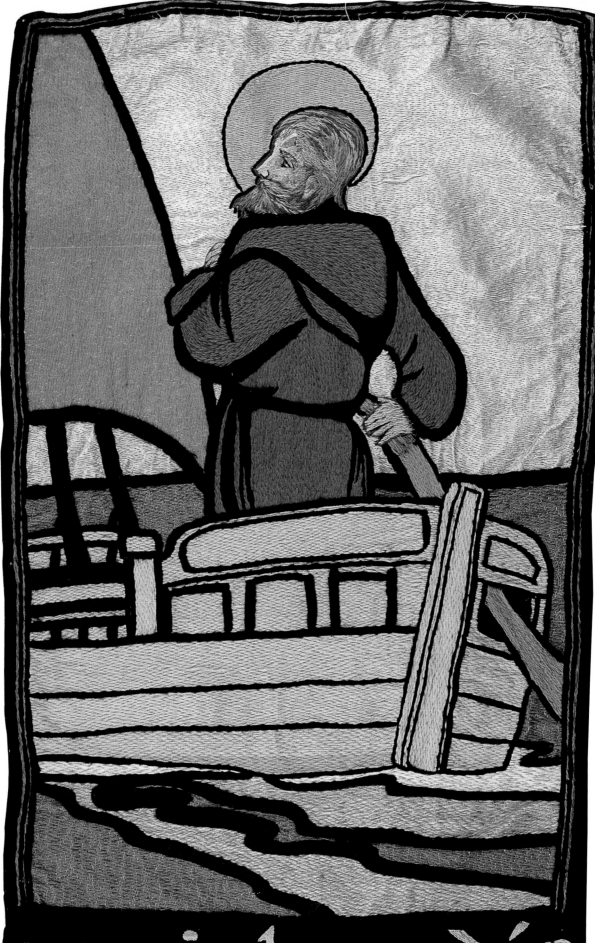

naom bneandán

THE DISTANT MAGNET
(1690–1840)

D rawn by ancient instincts and new opportunities, the Irish made America their new
destination of choice, once their vanguard
had helped to secure its independence from
Britain. The first generation of immigrants to
enter this new "United States" found it united
only in that it combined plenty of work with plenty of prejudice. Some
would succeed despite all odds, but many would become the pioneers of
the "American ghetto."

THE APPEAL OF AMERICA

The ancient Gaels had gazed out over the western ocean and fantasized
about "Hy Brasil," a paradise of eternal youth. Christian legends told of
Irish monks, led by the sixth-century missionary St. Brendan the Navigator,
crossing the Atlantic in wood and leather boats to preach the Gospel to red-
skinned congregations. Tradition insists that William Ayres, from Galway,
accompanied Columbus in 1492. More verifiable Irishmen certainly par-
ticipated in early English probes into the Western Hemisphere, from
Newfoundland in the north to Virginia in the south.

As permanent English colonies were established along the Atlantic seaboard
during the seventeenth century, Irish names appeared with increasing

*(Previous spread) The Cove
of Cork.* **Lithograph by
Currier & Ives.
Museum of the City of
New York. The Harry
T. Peters Collection.
Many Irish immigrants
departed from Cork.**

(Opposite) **Banner of St.
Brendan the Navigator
from St. Brendan's
Cathedral in Loughrea.
Brendan is believed to
have reached the shores
of America in the 6th
century A.D. and
preached the Gospel to
the first Americans.**

Daniel Boone leading pioneers through the Cumberland Gap into Kentucky in 1775. From a painting by George Caleb Bingham, 1851. Boone and his partners were typical of the Scotch-Irish pioneers who led the way in opening up the American frontier.

frequency among lists of settlers, soldiers, taxpayers, and transgressors. By 1690 an Irish-born witch was on trial in Massachusetts (speaking only Gaelic, which was at first mistaken for diabolic discourse). A military engineer in South Carolina was designing defense works and leaving his name on Sullivan's Island in Charleston Harbor. And in New York (which had a few stray Irish inhabitants even when it was the Dutch outpost of New Amsterdam), the Royal Governor Sir Thomas Dongan, from Limerick, urged his countrymen to settle in this fine, prosperous new colony.

Despite—or perhaps because of—the ambivalent relationship between England and Ireland, Irish immigration into the thirteen colonies grew steadily in the 1700s. Ulster Scots, fleeing the impact of restrictive trade practices on the nascent industries of Ireland's North, came in several waves. Towns with names like Londonderry and Bangor testify to their presence in New England. But many chose the back country of Virginia and the Carolinas, from which their sons would venture into the wilderness of Kentucky and Tennessee.

For other groups of immigrants, the appeal of America lay in its greater openness to religious dissent. Both the Presbyterian and Methodist churches were established in the New World by Irish settlers. The Quaker community of Pennsylvania also had strong Irish origins, growing from the Penn family's links to County Cork. Even Catholics found a degree of tolerance, if not complete sanctuary, in Maryland.

Whether seeking economic opportunity or religious latitude, the Irish in the colonies retained their ethnic identity, being singled out by other colonists (often pejoratively) as "Irish." They accepted the label proudly, making no distinction among Catholics, Anglicans, and "Scotch-Irish." As early as 1737, the Charitable Irish Society of Boston provided the model for fraternal and benevolent orders in New York and Philadelphia with names like Sons or Friendly Brothers of St. Patrick, and Hibernian Societies in Charleston and Baltimore.

While most among these early generations of Irish Americans toiled anonymously, a few attained prominence as servants of the Crown. In the role of Indian agent or frontier administrator, transplanted Celts such as George Croghan and James O'Hara brought their instinctive skill at coping with novel problems in exotic settings to the maintenance of law and order

A ewe grazing on a hillside of a misty island off the coast of Maine might well remind many new immigrants of what they left behind.

Arch Street in Philadelphia, 1799. Philadelphia was a major port of entry
and favorite residence for the earlier generations of Irish immigrants.

among the rough denizens of the borderlands. Preeminent for his achievements in this field was William Johnson. An immigrant who turned his youthful energy and a gift for "networking" into a major success story, Johnson became the king's representative to the Iroquois Confederacy, a baronet, a general, and a landed magnate in northern New York. A marriage alliance with the powerful chief of the Mohawks allowed Johnson to establish Irish settlers on the edge of Indian territory and to guard against French encroachments in the last of the great colonial wars for the control of North America. His son and nephew held the Iroquois in firm alliance to Britain during the Revolution and secured the Canadian border for the British Empire.

REVOLUTIONARIES AND REFUGEES

Not a few of the Irish in the thirteen colonies shared Sir William Johnson's loyalty to the British Crown. As tensions exploded into rebellion in 1775,

The Army and Navy. John Barry received his commission from George Washington. Barry was a native of Wexford and became one of the revolutionary navy's leading commanders, earning the designation "Father of the American Navy."

Boston Massacre, 1770. Among the five men killed in this clash between American demonstrators and British troops was Patrick Carr, a native of Ireland.

the American Irish seem to have been split, like the rest of the population, into three factions: one supporting the British regime, one seeking to remain neutral, and one taking up arms for independence. At least three regiments of loyalists were raised among Irish residents of the colonies, and one, the Volunteers of Ireland, so distinguished itself that it was soon incorporated into the British regular army.

Patriotic orators of a later day, however, preferred to recall that nearly a dozen signers of the Declaration of Independence were of Irish birth or extraction, while the secretary of the Continental Congress who registered it, the printer who ran off the first copies, and the officer who first read it to the assembled public were all born in Ireland. The Irish would also claim their martyrs, from Patrick Carr, who fell in the Boston Massacre, to Richard Montgomery, who died while commanding an American invasion of Canada. The O'Brien brothers of Maine led the first clashes with British sea power, and Commodore John Barry, from Wexford, earned the title "Father of the United States Navy." General John Sullivan destroyed the war-making power of the Iroquois, and Hercules Mulligan, a tailor, gathered intelligence for Washington's army in British-occupied New York, while Colonel Stephen Moylan and John Fitzgerald were key members of the commander-in-chief's staff. The European Wild Geese, too, spread their wings during the Revolutionary War, with the Franco-Irishmen Thomas

Conway and Stephen Roche, among others, lending their experience as generals in the Continental Army. When Spain entered the struggle on the rebel side, it was a contingent of her Irish brigade, under Colonel Arturo O'Neill, that drove the British out of Pensacola and undercut their position in Georgia.

Victory came in 1783 with Britain's recognition of the independence of the United States, and in the following year Irishmen in New York founded the Friendly Sons of St. Patrick. Uniting Anglicans, Presbyterians, and Catholics, as well as men who had taken differing positions in the recent conflict, the society symbolized, in what was already becoming the Irish-American capital, the solidarity and optimism of those who had now taken their stand in the new nation, without forgetting the old.

Scarcely had the American Revolution ended than the French Revolution began. Between 1789 and 1815, France, Britain, Ireland, and America were all drawn into a series of political upheavals and wars. The Society of United

The death of General Richard Montgomery during an American attack on Montreal in 1776. Montgomery was a native of Dublin and a former officer in the British army who had settled in the American colonies.

Old St. Patrick's Cathedral on Mott Street in lower Manhattan.
This early 19th-century church was the center
of Irish Catholic life in pre–Civil War New York.

Irishmen, with support from the new French Republic and sympathetic encouragement from American radicals, launched a rebellion in 1798 that began what became a two-hundred-year struggle for the end of British rule in Ireland. After this early failure, surviving "men of '98" made their way to the United States, to keep alive the flame of Irish nationalism. Conservatives, such as President John Adams, feared the disruptive influence of these refugees and sought, by such measures as the Alien and Sedition Acts, to protect Federalist equilibrium from these "Wild Irishmen." Thomas Jefferson's Democratic Party, on the contrary, welcomed these fellow revolutionaries and gave full scope to radical journalists like John Daly Burk or "rabble-rousing" politicians like Matthew Lyon, who won election to Congress from several states during his peripatetic and pugnacious career. After the Jeffersonians displaced the Federalists in 1801, a more sympathetic welcome was assured, even for Thomas Addis Emmet and William Macneven, who had been members of the United Irish Directory. Emmet, who became attorney general of New York State, Macneven, who became New York City health commissioner, and William Sampson, soon recognized as a leading light of the American Bar, were among those who added distinction to the growing Irish community. Nevertheless, these political refugees were abhorred by those Americans who saw nothing inconsistent

(Below, left) **Alexander Turney Stewart, a Scotch-Irish immigrant, became the founder of America's first department store in New York City, and one of the wealthiest men in this country. He was nominated for Secretary of the Treasury by President Grant.**

(Below, right) **Thomas Mellon, a Scotch-Irishman who joined the 1820's migration into western Pennsylvania, eventually became a judge and founded a fortune and a dynasty both still in evidence in 20th-century America.**

James W Shields, a general in the Mexican and Civil wars, and the only man to serve as a senator from three different states, Illinois, Minnesota, and Missouri.

in denouncing the Irish as blood-stained Jacobins while in the same breath condemning their supposed allegiance to papal monarchy. Americans of the "old stock" might indulge their fantasies and justify their prejudices by contradictory warnings of guillotines and "Popish tyranny," but most Irish immigrants of the early nineteenth century were more concerned with starting over than with starting a new regime. The promise of political and religious freedom appealed to "Papist" and "Protestant" alike. Even the idea of a British rather than an Irish nationality seemed less obnoxious once they had crossed the Atlantic. The Irish immigrants of this period not only ignored their own sectarian distinctions, but exchanged cordial greetings with the English, Scottish, and Welsh who had also braved the ocean crossing. It was common for Irish representatives to appear at St. George, St.

Mathew Carey, Philadephia publisher, bookseller, and scholar, was
a leading intellectual figure in
the pre–Civil War Irish-American
community.

Andrew, and St. David observances in New York City, and for delegates of other "British" ethnic societies to join in the March 17th celebrations of the Friendly Sons of St. Patrick.

The assimilation of the Irish into American society might have become a relatively smooth and speedy process, in spite of all the doubts and suspicions that met the refugees of the period, if only they had remained a modest minority. But numbers would change everything.

DREAMS FULFILLED, ILLUSIONS DISPELLED

During the Napoleonic Wars, Irish immigration to America had been little more than a trickle. After 1815, it became, if not yet a flood, then a steadily growing stream. In 1820, the first year which the United States kept a record of new Americans, 3,614 Irishmen and women entered the country.

The Erie Canal, constructed in the 1820s largely by Irish immigrant laborers, connected the upper Hudson River with the Great Lakes, providing the first major water access into the interior of North America, and contributing to the extension of the American frontier.

During the 1830s the annual rate averaged 18,000. Between 1820 and 1840, nearly 600,000 new Irish Americans were received at ports of entry ranging from New York and Boston to Savannah and New Orleans.

A few among these thousands would achieve fame, fortune, or both. The stories of four Ulsterman--two Protestant, two Catholic--may serve to illustrate the varieties of accomplishments possible for at least some of the Irish immigrants of the 1820s and 1830s.

Alexander T. Stewart, born near Belfast in 1803, worked his way up in the New York retail trade. Beginning as a teenage clerk, he became the founder of the first department store in the United States, a "splendid emporium" opposite City Hall. A philanthropist, railroad promoter, and projector of the planned community of Garden City on Long Island, he was eventually named Secretary of the Treasury by President Grant.

Thomas Mellon, from a farming village in County Tyrone, joined the second wave of "Scotch-Irish" immigration in the 1820s, settled in western Pennsylvania, became a judge, and established a line of merchants and bankers that, a century later, produced a Cabinet officer, a university benefactor, and a patron of the arts.

48

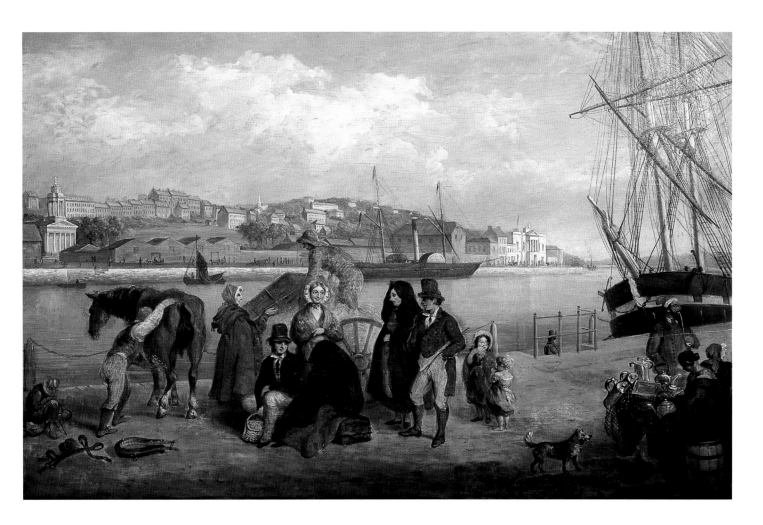

James Shields, another native of Tyrone, parlayed a flamboyant self-confidence into a political career that saw him, at various times, representing three different states in the U.S. Senate, and a military career that brought him to the rank of general of volunteers in both the Mexican and Civil wars.

John Hughes, one of the many priests sent from Ireland to serve a growing flock in America, became bishop, and then the first archbishop of New York. A dominant figure in his own Church, and a recognized political force in his city and state, he continued to play a major role in public affairs until his death in the 1860s.

Irish Americans could also boast of others who had achieved the dream of success in America, although in the cultural rather than the practical sphere. Mathew Carey, the scholar-publisher, Robert Walsh, the editor of literary journals, and Dominick Lynch, the promoter of classical music and

Emigrants at Cork. **Style of Nathaniel Grogan. c. 1820. Oil on canvas. Department of Irish Folklore, University College, Dublin.**

European opera in New York, were among those who displayed the aesthetic side of Irish character to their fellow Americans.

But for most immigrants, and their children, this was a time of dreams deferred. In the words of an oft-quoted Irish quip, "We came to America expecting to find the streets paved with gold. But they were not paved with gold; they were not paved at all; and we were expected to pave them." The majority of immigrants lived out their days in the new country paving those streets, digging ditches, and building mansions for other people to live in. It was the pick-and-shovel labor of Irish immigrants that built the Erie Canal in the 1820s, the waterway that opened up the interior of the nation to settlement. The Irish laid out the road network that became the first national highways, and laid down the track network for the first railways.

The Democrats facilitated the granting of citizenship to the immigrants, and Andrew Jackson ran for president with the boast that he was "an Irishman's son." But between elections the working-class Irish were far down on the scale of public esteem and acceptance. As more and more came to the United States, there seemed countless jobs for them to do, but little respect to spare. A few of them responded to the call of their eloquent compatriot, John L. O'Sullivan, the editor of the *Democratic Review,* who declared that it was America's "Manifest Destiny" to rule the whole continent. Some two hundred Irish families made their way to Texas, then under Mexican rule, and others, such as John MacLaughlin, went as far as the Oregon Territory. But the typical new arrival stayed on in the squalid slums of the great eastern seaboard cities, striving to keep his family alive, amid a resurgence of nativism.

During the 1830s recurrent outbursts of xenophobia led to the burning of a convent school near Boston, attacks on Catholic churches in Philadelphia, and anti-Irish riots in many towns. Only the staunch—and armed—resistance of Irish workmen in New York City spared their community buildings from similar destruction. Optimists declared that this, too, would pass, and proclaimed their confidence that "Native Americans" would, in God's own good time, get used to having the Irish among them. But worse was yet to come.

A CLOSER LOOK:
BEATING THE RUSH

The first Irish immigrants to America arrived in the early days of English colonial settlement. Two hundred years before the Famine influx, venturesome voyagers were "beating the rush."

In 1644, Daniel Gookin took up residence in Massachusetts, where he eventually became a member of the Governor's Council and major general of the militia.

In 1662, the town of Kinsale was founded in Virginia by Irish immigrants from County Cork.

In 1670 Irish settlers were among those who landed at Charleston, and founded the colony of South Carolina.

In 1672, Charles MacCarthy, from Cork, led a party of forty-eight Irish immigrants in the founding of East Greenwich, Rhode Island.

In 1680, George Talbot was granted an estate in Maryland which he named "New Ireland" and designated as a refuge for Irish settlers.

In 1682, Denis and Mary Rochford, from Wexford, accompanied William Penn on his first visit to Pennsylvania. Denis was elected a member of the Pennsylvania Assembly a year later.

In 1688, Anne Glover, a native of Ireland who had been sent as a slave to Barbados, and subsequently came to Massachusetts, was hanged in Boston. She had been convicted of witchcraft, following a trial in which her inability to speak English made it impossible to question her.

THE FAMINE ERA (1840–1860)

uring the late 1840s and early 1850s, the Irish people underwent the greatest trauma of their long, and often sorrowful, history. Famine and disease killed or drove more than a million men, women, and children overseas, and transferred the nation's posterity to the United States. The shock of their arrival left both the immigrants and their involuntary hosts disoriented and antagonistic. In time, an accommodation would evolve between the newcomers and the natives. But there would remain the lasting phenomenon of the Irish-American nationalist, who was committed to the idea that America was a westward extension of Ireland within which the refugees could rest, regroup, and work for the liberation of their ancestral homeland. For many Americans, this concept of a dual nationality was a novel and offensive doctrine. During the Famine era, the old ethnic and religious prejudices would be reinforced by accusations of divided loyalty.

THE GREAT HUNGER AND THE COFFIN SHIPS

It is the supreme irony in the convoluted study of Ireland's relationship with America that the catastrophe known as "The Famine" had an American root. Literally so, for the potato came to Ireland from America. This nutritious tuber was, according to tradition, transplanted from the

(Previous spread) Discovery of the Potato Blight. Department of Irish Folklore, University College, Dublin. The first signs of the fungus that destroyed Ireland's major subsistence crop were detected in the mid-1840s. By the end of the decade, hundreds of thousands had died or fled from Ireland.

(Opposite) Departure from Home. Wood engraving, from Harper's Weekly, June 26, 1859. Museum of the City of New York. Often the younger and more energetic members of Irish families were forced to leave parents and kinfolk behind with little prospect of seeing them ever again. The agony of the Famine era was intensified by the pain of these forced separations.

THE FAMINE IN IRELAND.—FUNERAL AT SKIBBEREEN.—FROM A SKETCH BY MR. H. SMITH, CORK.—(SEE NEXT PAGE.)

Funeral in Skibbereen.
The number of deaths in the most affected areas of the Famine overwhelmed the normal rituals surrounding death and burial and forced the Irish to use mass transport of corpses and mass burials.

Western Hemisphere to Sir Walter Raleigh's garden in Youghal, County Cork, at the end of the sixteenth century. In little over a hundred years it became a staple crop throughout Europe, nowhere more so than in Ireland, where the collapse of the old cattle-raising socioeconomic order had turned the peasantry into involuntary vegetarians. Other countries experienced crop loss from the onslaught of phylloxera and similar fungi during the eighteenth and early nineteenth centuries, but the dependence of the Irish masses on the potato as a single food source had already reached such a level by 1740 and 1741 that a "blight" in that year resulted in the starvation of well over one hundred thousand countryfolk.

Despite the precarious nature of its food-base, the population of Ireland grew steadily. The census of 1841 counted more than eight million residents, three-quarters of them tenant farmers or day laborers. Most of these subsisted on the easily cultivated potato, while the grains and other products of their labor were reserved for export. No alternative food source existed, nor, if it had, was there an adequate system for its distribution.

For decades, the dangerous demographics of Ireland had been ignored by a British administration whose laissez-faire principles created a policy of malign neglect, and by Irish politicians preoccupied with propaganda and parliamentary maneuvers. Daniel O'Connell, who had won Catholic emancipation (i.e., the removal of the last of the Penal Laws) in 1829, gloried in the title of "The Liberator" and focused his subsequent attentions on securing an autonomous legislature for Ireland. O'Connell created, during the course of his long career, Europe's first mass movement—a political organization based on the mobilization of the common people of Ireland, who paid a shilling a year to fund newspapers and agitators, and who turned out in the tens of thousands for marches, rallies, and "monster meetings." Thanks to O'Connell and the British constitutional traditions of electoral choice and representative bodies, the Irish would come to America with a deeper knowledge of the democratic process than most other major immigrant groups. But "The Liberator" and his adversaries remained equally oblivious to Ireland's real, and most urgent problem: the sustenance of its ever-swelling population.

By 1846, after a series of political reverses, and with his health in decline, O'Connell faced a revolt from within his party ranks by the "Young Ireland" movement. These dissidents, who favored a return to the violent tactics of an earlier day, would launch an abortive rebellion in 1848 and renew the cause of revolutionary nationalism in the United States. But as

Daniel O'Connell addresses a gathering of Repeal Association supporters at Clifden in the Irish Highlands, March 1843. These "monster meetings" were typical of O'Connell's tactics in mobilizing his mass following to force "peaceful" change on the structure of British rule in Ireland.

Contemporary engraving of impoverished farmers in County Kildare. These were the potential immigrants of the Famine era who had no prospects or even a chance of survival if they stayed in Ireland.

O'Connell set off on the pilgrimage to Rome that would be his last journey, all of these considerations were about to become irrelevant. The potato blight had come again.

From 1846 through 1848, Ireland's potato crop was destroyed, in whole or in part, by a pervasive fungus. By 1847—"Black '47"—famine was widespread, disease (including typhus and cholera) was reaching epidemic proportions, and Irish society was collapsing. Relief and medical services were inadequate, or, in many areas, nonexistent. Government response was minimal, crippled by its doctrinaire insistence upon allowing natural socioeconomic forces to run their course, and a refusal to burden the British taxpayer with the cost of remedying Irish ills. Private charity, whether it came from religious or secular sources, was soon overwhelmed by the magnitude of the crisis, though supplemented by European—and even American—contributions.

As the "Great Hunger" tightened its grip, flight became the only option for those who did not want to join the "starving wretches" hopelessly plucking grass from the fields and bark from the trees. Scraping together their meager resources, they bought passage on the vessels that advertised in every port of transatlantic salvation. For those who lacked the money, landlords, eager to rid their estates of human encumbrances, would often pay the way of whole parties of tenants, whose vacated cottages would be replaced by sheep runs or cattle pens.

Whether departing directly from Irish harbors, or sailing first to Britain, the refugees were compelled to make the month-long ocean crossing under conditions of desperate adversity. Obliged to provide their own food for the passage, they often experienced a new round of famine as supplies ran short when storms and adverse winds extended their time at sea. Crowded, unsanitary passenger holds, recurrent outbreaks of disease, and cumulative effects of exhaustion took their toll on these "coffin ships." Survivors of the voyage to America had, in many cases, seen aged parents or infants buried at sea during the flight to their supposed land of salvation.

Whole shiploads of Irish immigrants had to be placed in quarantine when they reached America. Those heading for Canada were usually detained at Grosse Isle in the St. Lawrence River, where thousands died of "ship fever" without ever setting foot in the "Promised Land." The quarantine station at Staten Island, which served the port of New York, became so feared as a "pesthole" by the local residents that they burned it down.

By the time the Great Hunger came to an end in 1849, an estimated 1,000,000 inhabitants of Ireland had died of starvation and disease. The

This illustration from *Frank Leslie's Illustrated Newspaper* of 1856 shows the continuation of the flight from Ireland that began during the peak year of the Famine. The rate of emigration did not diminish until the eve of the Civil War.

A.B. Houghton. *Between Decks in an Emigrant Ship.* Print. The Metropolitan Museum of Art,
Harris Brisbane Dick Fund, 1928. The crowded, unsanitary conditions for steerage passengers
in transatlantic immigrant ships moderated only slightly from the 1840s down through the 1870s.

massive dislocation of Ireland's population continued to be felt, however, as the flow of refugees overseas lasted throughout the 1850s. Apart from those who fled to Britain itself, or the far corners of the British Empire, more than 1,700,000 immigrants entered the United States during the 1840–1860 Famine era. During the peak year of 1852, over 219,000 sought sanctuary, to say nothing of those who crossed, unrecorded, from Canada.

For Ireland, the Famine era meant a shrinkage of population from eight million in 1841 to four million in 1901. In addition to the demographic catastrophe, the Famine precipitated a socioeconomic revolution in Ireland and the near extinction of the traditional Gaelic culture.

For the United States, the Famine era marked the beginning of Irish America.

ALIEN NATION

Before the Famine era, Anglo-Americans had thought of the Irish as dwellers on Britain's Celtic fringe whose representatives in the United States could be treated with the same dismissive contempt or—less frequently—grateful respect, shown to the Irish "at home." Now, the Irish were upon them, by the thousands—and hundreds of thousands. At first, the pitiable condition in which the refugees from the Famine arrived might evoke a certain compassion or even grudging acceptance. But as the crisis in Ireland eased and the immigrants continued to pour into the United States, tolerance changed to antagonism, then to fear.

The quarantine station at Staten Island, 1857, one of a number of detention facilities where "sick and diseased" immigrants were held for medical observation. Some of these stations were attacked and burned down by fearful residents of the area.

Samuel B. Waugh. *The Bay and Harbor of New York.* c. 1855. Oil on canvas. Museum of the City of New York, gift of Mrs. Robert Littlejohn. Castle Garden immigration station (in the background) was the first site of their new home for many Irish immigrants who not only landed in but remained in New York City.

Scene in the Five Points district in lower Manhattan. During the Famine era and well beyond the Civil War this slum area just north of City Hall was proverbial for squalor, vice, and drink-related establishments.

To a country still essentially homogeneous in its population (if one disregarded—as most Americans did—Indians and blacks), the new Irish immigrants seemed profoundly alien. Often speaking little or no English, uneducated, unskilled in anything but the most basic manual labor, unaccustomed to urban ways, yet springing from a level of peasantry more primitive than most American farmers knew, frequently addicted to strong drink and brutal brawling, uncouth and Catholic, the Irish were a separate nation, obviously quite incapable of ever integrating into the American nation.

The Irish were forced by poverty and prejudice to live apart in the crumbling waterfront slums of Boston, the squalid Five Points district north of New York's City Hall, where "crime, vice, and violence flourished" and—much farther north in Manhattan—the isolated "Nanny Goat Hill" (destined to be swept away in the 1850s for the construction of Central Park). In these and similar ghettos, "the Irishmen and his disgusting domestic companion, the pig" were alleged to live a subhuman existence, portrayed in contemporary illustrations as an endless round of drunken "Donnybrooks." Artists did not hesitate to emphasize "simian" features or convey a pervasive look of low cunning mixed with bestial ferocity.

Having thus branded the immigrants as outcasts, Anglo-American society stigmatized them as clannish foreigners who preferred their own kind to the mainstream of American life. The Irish were thus simultaneously rejected, and condemned as standoffish.

NEW YORK IN 1855.

New York street scene in 1855.

Enlistment of Irish and German immigrants for Civil War service. Many of these new arrivals were induced to join up for war immediately upon landing in New York City, often without any idea of what the Civil War was all about.

Thus stereotyped and prejudged, it was useless for the immigrants to apply for jobs that involved more than a strong back and a willingness to work long hours for low wages. They were the pick-and-shovel men and the dock laborers of antebellum America, competing with the free blacks of the North and the slave labor of the South for the menial tasks of a prospering economy.

Some of the immigrants took the classic alternative of the socially marginalized—enlistment in the army. Even there, however, their path was not smooth. During the War with Mexico (1846–1848), deserters from the United States forces enlisted under the Mexican banner and fought against their former comrades. The Mexicans formed them into "St. Patrick's Batallion," and reported that they had chosen to join Catholic Mexico's struggle after experiencing religious discrimination from the Yankees. Not all of the deserters were Irish, and the truth of their motives is unclear. But some died in combat and others were executed after being captured, named as traitors to their adopted country. This episode of the "San Patricios" confirmed the opinion of many Anglo-Americans that the Irish were an alien nation, in, but not of, the United States.

66

Jamie & the Bishop.
Colored lithograph.
The Irish Catholic
immigrant comes to
the aid of his bishop
who is being assailed
by Scotch Protestant
"bigots."

"AMERICAN" OR "IRISH"?

"Go West, young man!" said Horace Greeley. The celebrated journalist (himself of Irish descent) was not specifically addressing his exhortation to the new immigrants, but the boldest among them took his advice. While Irish footprints had been left on western trails in earlier days, the great annexations after the Mexican War opened up great new stretches of land to exploitation. It was an Irishman who made the initial gold "strike" in California (though he kept none of it), and the Gold Rush of the late 1840s drew what one writer described as "a considerable Hibernian

Irish immigrants left
the confinement of
Eastern towns to follow
their destiny in the
wild West, finding
employment as loggers,
miners, railroad work-
ers, and anything else
one could dream of.

James Fair, one of the "self-made" men who rose from the ranks of Irish immigrants and made his fortune in the Nevada silver mines.

element." By the mid-1850s, with California already a state, the Irish of San Francisco and Sacramento had the satisfaction of seeing compatriots in the governor's chair and the senate. Nevada's bonanza was the silver mining boom at the end of the 1850s, and here again, Irish immigrants who had trekked across the "Great American Desert" or sailed all the way around to the Pacific coast, were heavily involved, whether they suffered claim-jumping and murder, like Eugene and Jeremiah O'Sullivan, or "struck it rich," like John MacKay and James Fair.

"Going West" for the immigrants meant not merely opportunity, but also escape from the rigid social structure and "established standards" that had already become solidified in the "civilized" East. Life on the ever-westward-moving frontier was more freewheeling and tolerant, allowing newcomers to pursue "a career open to talent." Nor was it necessary to traverse the Rockies. Chicago, no more than a trading post in the 1830s, was a thriving town only twenty years later, and the Irish were already laying the basis for their distinctive local institutions.

It was not the adaptation of the Chicago Irish to American life, however, that attracted the most attention in 1859. It was, rather, their hosting of a "congress" of refugees that proclaimed the establishment of an Irish Republic—a government in exile, complete with president, cabinet, elaborately printed bonds, and a commitment to liberate Ireland. This grandiose gesture marked the revival of the failed Young Ireland movement in the form of the Irish Republican Brotherhood, commonly known (after an ancient Irish warrior order) as the Fenians.

Here, indeed, was an "alien nation" in the heart of the "American nation." Not only did these immigrants sing songs about the "old country," and cling to their outlandish foreign ways, they now presumed to erect a

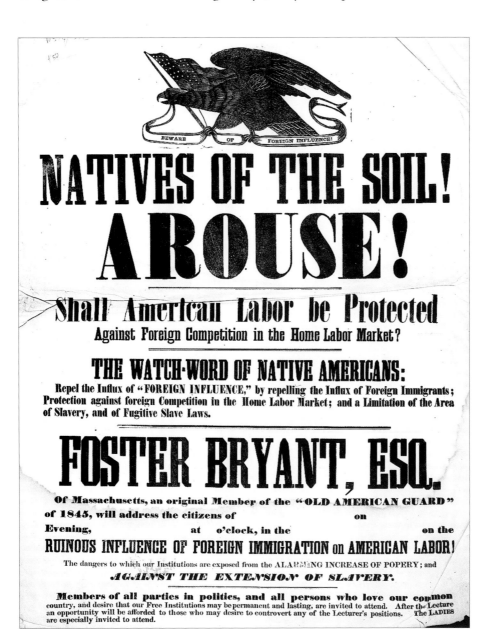

A nativist poster of the Famine era warning "Native-born" Americans against the dangers of immigration, which threatens to overwhelm the Protestant Anglo-American population in a sea of foreign Catholics.

THE FENIAN BANNER.

A Fenian banner of 1866 pays tribute to Grattan, Emmet, and O'Connell, joining together Irish leaders whose actual principles were quite divergent but who had entered into the pantheon of Irish nationalism. Lithograph, 1866.

provisional government for their erstwhile residence in the heart of America and began to raise money to carry on a revolutionary struggle abroad.

Nor could the "Irish Republic" be dismissed as mere rhetorical moonshine. In those places where they were most numerous, the immigrants had flocked into the nearly moribund state militia system, filling up existing regiments or even creating new ones. Such units displayed the green harp–emblazoned banner of Ireland alongside the Stars and Stripes, and the Fenian masterminds who had orchestrated this process clearly intended to co-opt a sizable part of the country's militia as a training ground—if not in actual combat force—for the projected Irish Republican Army. When, in 1860, the Prince of Wales visited New York, the 69th Regiment refused to participate in a review honoring Queen Victoria's heir. Colonel Michael Corcoran (a one-time policeman in Ireland) was summoned to face court-martial for this "mutinous" gesture, but the deeper issue remained: Just whose army was it anyway?

The 1850s saw a new, intense burst of nativism that was provoked by the immigrants' seeming ambivalence over patriotic loyalties. The old motives of religious and ethnic prejudice were superseded by political passions. Groups such as the "Native American Party" and the "National Republican Party" demanded restrictions on immigration and a twenty-one-year residency requirement before citizenship could be obtained.

For those who adhered to the Fenian program, with its secret links to revolutionary cadres in Ireland and its dream of breaking the hated "British chains," there was no inconsistency between their love of the "old coun-try" and their allegiance to the new. They thought of Ireland and America as a continuum, with the western half of the great transatlantic realm as a place in which they could find the time and the resources to regroup for the continuation of their crusade to make Ireland just as free and prosper-ous as the United States had become through its own defeat of British colonialism.

Most of the country's "old stock" inhabitants, even if they had understood this artful argument, would have dismissed it as absurd. For them the ques-tion was simple: Are you "American" *or* "Irish"?

Nicolino Calyo. *The Milk Man.* c. 1840–44. Watercolor. Museum of the City of New York, gift of Mrs. Francis P. Garyan in memory of Francis P. Garyan.

The Milk Man

Welcome to the land of freedom. An ocean steamer carrying immigrants passing the Statue of Liberty. Colored engraving. 19th century.

AMERICA LEARNS TO COPE WITH THE IRISH (1860–1890)

When Abraham Lincoln's election split the Union and precipitated the great Civil War, the Irish were still regarded by most Americans as a problem, if not an outright menace. During the next three decades, the country learned how to cope with these peculiar, but increasingly useful, strangers in their midst. In each of the three great regions that comprised the United States, the Irish helped shape late nineteenth-century America. In the South, they crushed secession and slavery. In the West, they tamed the Indians, conquered the wilderness, and exploited the land's resources. In the North, they built the infrastructure and the institutions of the great cities. By 1890, the Irish fitted into the American scene.

PROVING THEIR LOYALTY: THE IRISH IN THE CIVIL WAR

In the great war that split the country from 1861 to 1865, the Irish rallied dramatically to the Union cause. To be sure, the Confederacy had its supporters among the comparatively small number of immigrants who had settled in the South. Stephen Mallory, an ex-senator from Florida, the son of an Irish washerwoman, was Secretary of the Navy. John Mitchel, a one-time leader of the Young Irelanders, propagandized for the Confederates,

(Previous spread) St. Patrick's Day in America, Union Square. Early 1870s. Colored lithograph. Museum of the City of New York, The J. Clarence Davies Collection. This representation of a New York St. Patrick's Day parade in the late 19th century is in many respects more symbolic than representational.

(Opposite) Ulysses S. Grant as commander of the victorious Union army. Grant was a hero to the thousands of Union soldiers he led to victory in the Civil War.

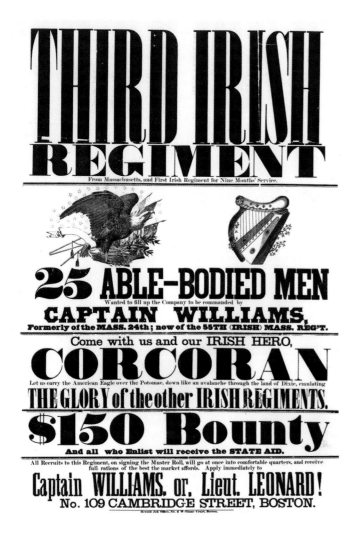

THIRD IRISH REGIMENT

From Massachusetts, and First Irish Regiment for Nine Months' Service.

25 ABLE-BODIED MEN

Wanted to fill up the Company to be commanded by

CAPTAIN WILLIAMS,

Formerly of the MASS. 24th; now of the 55TH (IRISH) MASS. REG'T.

Come with us and our IRISH HERO,

CORCORAN

Let us carry the American Eagle over the Potomac, down like an avalanche through the land of Dixie, emulating

THE GLORY of the other IRISH REGIMENTS.

$150 Bounty

And all who Enlist will receive the STATE AID.

All Recruits to this Regiment, on signing the Muster Roll, will go at once into comfortable quarters, and receive full rations of the best the market affords. Apply immediately to

Captain WILLIAMS, or, Lieut. LEONARD!

No. 109 CAMBRIDGE STREET, BOSTON.

A recruiting poster for a Massachusetts regiment, one of the many Irish regiments in the Union army.

and two of his sons gave their lives for the cause. Patrick Cleburne, who had journeyed from Cork to Arkansas, was one of three Irish-born generals in gray, and attained the highest praise for his military skills before falling in battle in 1864. Here and there—in Savannah, Mobile, and New Orleans—companies of "rebel" volunteers proclaimed themselves as proudly all Irish.

All this was nothing, however, compared to the more than 150,000 men of Irish birth—including twelve generals—who fought to restore the unity of their adopted country. Reinforced by the sons and grandsons of immigrants, these Celtic warriors formed whole brigades of volunteers, swelling the ranks of the entire Union army. But most dramatically visible were the exclusively Irish regiments raised in New York, Massachusetts, Pennsylvania, Illinois, and other states. The recruiting posters, of course, often bore those not-too-subtle references to serving Ireland at some future date, but not even nativists could deny that the Irish soldiers' prime obligation was the destruction of the Confederate Rebellion.

Any doubts about the loyalty of the immigrants were swept away by their valor in a hundred battles, from Bull Run, Antietam, and Gettysburg, to final campaigns in Georgia and northern Virginia. The repeated attacks by the Irish troops against Confederate entrenchments on the heights of Fredericksburg won the astonished admiration of friend and foe alike. "There could be no question of the dedication and patriotism of men as brave as these," wrote one observer. Michael Corcoran, not long before

menaced with dismissal for insulting an English prince, died as commander of the Irish brigade formed around his "Fighting 69th," and was succeeded by Thomas Francis Meagher, the most spectacular of these Irish
defenders of the Union. "Meagher of the Sword," as he was known for his
advocacy of armed revolution, had been condemned for treason after the
Young Ireland rising in 1848, then escaped from Tasmanian banishment to
become a lawyer and nationally renowned orator in the United States. For
all his championing of Irish nationalism, Meagher's war record established
his American credentials, and he was serving as governor of the Montana
Territory at the time of his death.

Just as flamboyant in action as Meagher, though more modest in
demeanor, was Philip Sheridan. There was some dispute over whether
"Little Phil" was born in Ireland or in America, but there was no debate
over his achievements as a leader of cavalry. "I used to think you were too
short to be a good horse soldier," Lincoln declared, "but now I know that
you're just the right size!" After the war, Sheridan would continue his

**The Irish Brigade
chaplains and officers
at Harrison's Landing,
Virginia, prior to their
departure for Antietam.
William Corby, chap-
lain of the 88th New
York, is seated on
the right.**

A CLOSER LOOK:
THE FIGHTING 69TH

The 69th Infantry Regiment of the New York State Militia was born out of the Famine-era flood of Irish immigrants, and their desire to serve their new country while preserving their ties to the old. Like other militia units formed during the 1850s in areas of major Irish settlement, this New York City–based regiment displayed the traditional banner of Ireland—a gold harp on a green field—alongside the state and national flags. Its sympathies with the oppressed homeland were demonstrated when its colonel, Michael Corcoran, refused to take part in an 1860 parade honoring the visiting Prince of Wales.

Such matters were overshadowed by the outbreak of the Civil War in 1861. The 69th, which formed the nucleus of the Irish Brigade, fought throughout the war, taking a notable part in the battles of Bull Run, Fair Oaks, Antietam, Chancellorsville, and Gettysburg. Its repeated assaults on the Confederate entrenchments atop Maryes' Heights at Fredericksburg won tributes for dauntless gallantry from both armies. The regiment's successive commanders, Michael Corcoran and Thomas F. Meagher, were (like most of their soldiers) immigrants demonstrating that they were "true Americans." Both attained the rank of general, as well as a reputation for speaking their minds.

The "Fighting 69th" won further fame (and inspired a Hollywood film) in the First World War, under Colonel "Wild Bill" Donovan (later the founder of the OSS, the CIA's forerunner).

The 69th took part in the Pacific campaigns of the Second World War, and has remained active in the National Guard.

Don Troiani. *Sons of Erin.* **Oil on canvas. While General Meagher brandishes his sword to lead the advance of the Irish Brigade toward Bloody Lane, Chaplain William Corby rides along the line, giving absolution to the men. Before this battle Meagher reminded his men to "Remember Ireland and Fontenoy" and the Wild Geese who fought so valiantly before them.**

(Left) The Irish Brigade played a pivotal role in the battle of Antietam—the single bloodiest day in the Civil War. On the front of the Irish Brigade Monument, erected in October 1997 at Antietam National Battlefield in Maryland, is depicted the advance of the 69th color guard and the transference of the colors from the fallen flag bearer to the running soldier The massive bas relief by sculptor Ron Tunison is supported by granite imported from County Down.

(Below) Sculptor Ron Tunison at work in his studio on a clay model of General Thomas Francis Meagher for the reverse side of the Irish Brigade Monument at Antietam.

Rare photo of Mathew Brady taken in his studio July 22, 1861, after Brady returned from Bull Run.

Soldiers at the ready surround the famed "Mortar Dictator" at Petersburg.

career to the very pinnacle, as he ended his days as commanding general of the United States Army.

Even more important than their bravery in battle in winning acceptance for the Irish was the simple fact of their service. By sharing the common experience of those who fought for the nation's preservation, the newcomers formed bonds of comradeship and shared hardships. As their brothers-in-arms learned to know them, amidst the grandeurs and miseries of military life, these fellow soldiers became fellow citizens.

For Civil War veterans and their families, the Irish had proved their loyalty and demonstrated their humanity. It was now possible to get beyond stereotypes and prejudices, and to deal with Irish immigrants and their descendants as individuals rather than an indistinguishable horde of transients.

Allowances still had to be made for negative behavior. The New York draft riots of 1863, marked by murderous violence and savage vandalism, were widely blamed on uncontrollable "Hibernian passions." More generous observers, however, interpreted these anticonscription outbursts in socioeconomic rather than ethnic terms, noting that the rioters were drawn from various components of the working class and were venting their proletarian rage on a system that permitted well-to-do New Yorkers whose names were drawn in the draft lottery to pay for a substitute, at a fee that an ordinary laborer could not afford. By making the conflict into "a rich man's war and a poor man's fight," the Federal authorities gave some justification to the "armies of the street" and to the Irish part in the riots.

Even more trying to the patience of their fellow Americans was the Irish invasion of Canada. In 1866, the Fenian-led Irish Republican Army, composed of several thousand Civil War veterans, crossed from northern New York into Ontario, with the intention of holding Canada for ransom, the aim being Britain's withdrawal from Ireland. The seasoned fighters of the Fenian force routed the raw militia that stood against them, but were compelled to abandon their grand design when Washington bowed to British protests and threatened to intervene unless the "Irish Republic" desisted. A smaller raid, launched from Vermont in 1870, was easily defeated by a better-prepared British garrison.

The nativists of the 1850s might well have pointed to the Canadian affair as proof that the true loyalty of the Irish lay elsewhere. In reality, the

(Left) **Major General Philip Henry Sheridan, the most famous "Irish" soldier of the Civil War, a redoubtable cavalry commander and hero of his immigrant followers.**

(Following spread) **Mathew Brady, at right leaning against a tree, takes a closer look at the battlefield.**

majority of those who followed the course of this bizarre adventure in the press evidently found it more entertaining than scandalous. In their very grandiosity, the Fenian's schemes had more of P.T. Barnum than Benedict Arnold about them. What might in the past have been called treason, was now dismissed as mere eccentricity or self-dramatization.

The charge that the Irish were "hyphenated Americans" would be raised again in the years to come, but after the Civil War, the peculiar idea that one could be *both* "American" and "Irish" found general acceptance. The "alien nation" had been absorbed into the United States.

PROVING THEIR USEFULNESS:
THE IRISH IN THE WINNING OF THE WEST

Mathew Brady, the most famous and popular photographer of the Civil War era. His battlefield scenes brought the war home to the civilian population.

With the War Between the States finally brought to an end, the reunited nation resumed the great enterprise of winning the West, with the Irish as eager participants. For every ex-soldier who contemplated the invasion of Canada, a hundred made their way west. For every Irishman who had ventured into the wilderness before the war, a thousand now left the crammed

confines of the East to pursue their fortunes in the wide-open spaces across the Mississippi.

The prime symbol of postwar optimism and expansion in the West was the transcontinental railroad. The dream of linking the Atlantic with the Pacific had been transformed into a real plan and real construction before the war, with the Central Pacific line being pushed eastward over the Rockies, while the Union Pacific company undertook the thrust westward across the Great Plains. To this latter task, thousands of Irish veterans lent their enthusiasm and energy between 1865 and 1869.

As they laid track, drove spikes, bridged streams, and shored up embankments, the railroad workers often had to discard their tools and snatch up rifles to beat off attacks by Indians. Over a thousand miles of storms, floods, and savagery, "Poor Paddy worked on the railroads," driving the Union Pacific ever westward until it joined its sister line in the wilds of Utah, and the continent was spanned. Like the immigrants of an earlier

This photograph by Timothy O'Sullivan, one of Mathew Brady's assistants, is a scene from the aftermath of the Battle of Gettysburg, 1863.

generation who built the canals and roads of the emerging United States, the Irishmen who completed the transcontinental railroad—and the many lines that branched out from it across the western territories—often put down roots in this new environment, transforming railhead camps into the towns that would in turn become cities. In these newly created settings, the Irish would be founding fathers rather than beggars at the back door. Irish immigrants liked to tell the story of a "greenhorn" (always from some county other than their own) who arrived in New York during the war and signed up immediately for a job in which he would wear a fine blue uniform, only to discover that he was not going to be a street-car conductor but, rather, an infantryman. Unlike this apocryphal simpleton, a host of wartime immigrants enlisted, fully aware that they were going off to battle. The martial spirit had impelled the Celts over many centuries, and even after the great Civil War was over, the U.S. Army continued to recruit a disproportionate number of Irishmen.

The department of the West, under the command of General Philip Sheridan, was the venue for the army's struggle with the aboriginal inhabitants of America that finally closed the frontier era. The Irish, from Sheridan on down, added their distinctive flavor to these operations, whether it was reflected in Custer's choice of "Garryowen" as the regimental march of the 7th Cavalry, or the soldiers' rueful ballads about the harsh discipline of "Sergeant John McCafferty and Captain Donohue." Individual heroes like Myles Keogh of Little Bighorn fame, who evoked the old "Wild Geese" image of adventure, or the Murphys and Kellys, who relentlessly pursued renegade Sioux and Apaches, were celebrated in "dime-store novels" and eastern newspapers as the gallant constabulary who made the West safe for civilians. The Indian-fighting Irish soldier, in the two decades after Appomattox, became the respected and reliable "winner of the West."

Farmers and herdsmen for centuries in the Old World, the Irish in the West did not, as a rule, take to "sod-busting" or ranching. Some of them undoubtedly did become farmers or cowboys, but the large scale, isolated holdings, and the loneliness of these occupations generally did not appeal

A shanty town at Dale Creek Bridge housing predominately Irish railroad workers on the route of the transcontinental railroad during the post–Civil War era.

Sections of the transcontinental railroad:
Carmichael's Cut in Granite Canyon *(top)*,
and Malloy's Cut *(bottom)*.

to the Celtic psyche. A sociable people, accustomed to having neighbors and kinfolk at hand, they could not adjust to being fifty or a hundred miles from the nearest town, or even from the nearest homestead. The Irish were much more in evidence on the mining frontier. While their compatriots were wresting coal and iron from the hills of Pennsylvania and Minnesota, the gold mines of Colorado and the copper mines of Montana drew Irish "diggers" by the thousands. Cities like Denver and Butte became outposts of the Celtic diaspora, and Irish miners became pioneers of the labor movement of the West.

The Irish presence in the West was not entirely benign. Sociability sometimes gave way to antisocial behavior that would have confirmed the worst fears of 1840's nativists. In the tumultuous atmosphere of the time and place, it is hardly surprising that individual criminals, or even whole gangs of bandits, like the murderous Daltons, took advantage of the West's wildness. The Irishness of Henry Carty, a New York street tough turned New Mexico gunman, was disguised under the nickname of "Billy the Kid"—nor was he the only killer of Irish origin involved in the bloody business of settling the Southwest. Yet, there were Irish-American lawmen, too, and it was Sheriff Patrick Garrett who finally gunned down the supposedly invincible "Kid" in 1881. As in the best western movies, the white hats triumphed over the black hats in the final reel.

(Above) A dormitory car for Irish railroad workers, 1880s.

(Below) Billy the Kid, originally named Henry Carty, was an Irish-American street tough from New York who killed his way to notoriety in the New Mexico Territory during the Civil War period.

The Erin Go Bragh Saloon, Duluth, Minnesota, c. 1875. By this period large numbers of Irish immigrants had settled in the Great Lakes area, including Minnesota, a state generally associated with Scandinavian immigration.

STEAM SHOVEL, COPPER FLAT.
Mc GILL, NEVADA.

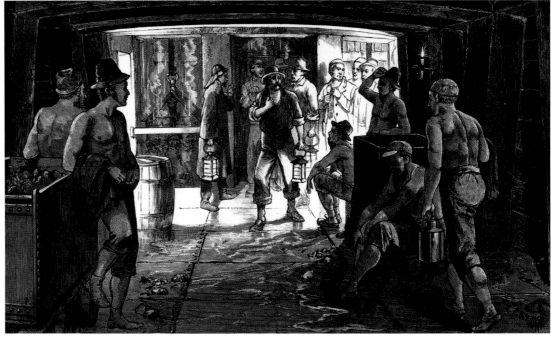

(Above) Steam shovel. Copper flat. McGill, Nevada. Many Irish miners were employed in the silver and copper mines in this region.

(Right) Scene in a silver mine at Virginia City, Nevada. Venturesome Irish immigrants were among the earliest to respond to the silver strike in the 1850s, and continued to work the mines through the Civil War period.

PROVING THEIR VALUE:
THE IRISH IN THE SHAPING OF URBAN AMERICA

Visible though they might be on southern battlefields and western fron-
tiers, the Irish were still perceived, during the post–Civil War era, as city-
dwellers in the North—a region encompassing New England, the Middle
Atlantic states, and the Great Lakes area. Between 1860 and 1890, an average of 60,000 immigrants a year arrived from Ireland, and most of these
continued to settle in urban agglomerations east of the Mississippi and
north of the Mason-Dixon line.

As early as 1870, the Irish-born population of New York City was 202,000
out of a total of 942,000. The neighboring, but then independent, city of
Brooklyn had over 96,000 immigrants in a population of some 340,000.
New York was already being called "The Irish Capital of the World," but
many other cities in the region, including Boston, Philadelphia, Baltimore,
Chicago, and Cincinnati, counted 20 to 30 percent of Irish birth among
their residents. Most of these immigrants, and their children, still lived in
localities, often called "Irishtown," that were in transition from outright
ghettos to comfortably ethnic enclaves. Their occupations, too, were in
transition.

The Irish were not only living in these steadily growing American cities,
they were building them. Irish construction workers, whose predecessors
had literally paved the unpaved streets, were now laying the tramcar lines
that ran alongside them, raising the elevated railroad lines that ran above
them, and the first stages of the subway that would stretch beneath. Other
Irish immigrants, or their sons, would become the motormen and the
conductors of these urban transit networks. Not far beyond loomed the
spectre of automobile traffic jams, for Henry Ford, the son of a Famine era
immigrant, was already contemplating his motorcar's assault upon urban as
well as rural roadways.

The skyscraper made its appearance on the American scene thanks to the
architectural genius of Louis Sullivan, another immigrant's son, and the

Irish provided the muscle and the skill that reared even taller structures that soared above the cities' streets. Their work included, of course, not only office towers, but the tenements in which they and successive generations of immigrants from other countries would live. The 1880s would also see the rise of such awesome examples of urban monument building as the Statue of Liberty and the Brooklyn Bridge.

The Irish were, too, in a metaphorical as well as a physical sense, builders of another great American urban institution of the late nineteenth century. "The Roman Catholic Church in the United States is actually the Irish Catholic Church," one less-than-enchanted observer maintained. In truth, whatever mixed English, French, and Spanish origins the Church might have exhibited in its missionary days, it had become synonymous with the Irish in most Americans' minds. Priests and bishops had been dispatched to the New World to provide spiritual sustenance and guidance to the rising flow of Irish immigrants even before the great tide of the Famine era. A framework of dioceses and parishes was filled in by an institutional

The Construction of the Brooklyn Bridge. 1877. Museum of the City of New York. Irish labor was of major consequence in erecting this great monument to urban growth and pride in late 19th-century America.

97

St. Patrick's Day in America. 1872. Colored lithograph. This symbolic representation of an Irish-American Civil War veteran and the crossed flags of the two countries succinctly illustrates the special relationship to Irish national aspirations still felt by many immigrants of the period.

Irish Clam diggers
Boston Mass 1882.

Irish Clam Diggers, Boston, 1882. The Boston Irish retained their strong working-class identity through-out a period of intense social mobility among the Irish in other parts of the country.

tapestry of schools and colleges, hospitals and orphanages, convents and seminaries, to provide Catholics with what they might otherwise lack— and to secure them against the encroachment of "Protestantism or indifference." So thoroughly was this massive system of religious facilities identified with the predominant group of Catholics, and so completely was its clergy dominated by those of Irish birth or ancestry, that few both-ered to distinguish between the Church and its institutions and the ethnic group that filled its ranks. The Church, like the Irish, was most visible in the big city, and its structures were correspondingly big, none more so than the towering cathedrals that combined the Gothic tradition of grandeur with a desire to assert status and legitimacy on the American stage. These ornaments of urban America included New York's St. Patrick's Cathedral (completed in 1879), which became a municipal landmark and focus of civil as well as religious rituals.

Yet it was not the cardinals and archbishops of the Catholic hierarchy, nor even rich businessmen, like the shipping magnate (and New York mayor) W.R. Grace, or the midwestern meat-packing family, the Cudahys, or the

(Above) The Great Chicago Fire of 1871. The prevalence of Irish immigrant settlers in Chicago and a readiness to blame them for all of the city's misfortunes is illustrated by the story that this destructive blaze was caused by "Mrs. O'Leary's cow" (right).

Dedication ceremonies for the Statue of Liberty, 1886. Irish workers laid the foundation and built the base upon which this French gift to America rested.

financier (and art gallery patron) W.W. Corcoran of Washington, who most clearly demonstrated the role of the Irish immigrant in the shaping of urban America. It was, rather, the leaders of Tammany Hall. These "bosses" of the New York Democratic Party created a political machine during the 1880s that came into full operation by the turn of the century and provided a model for the rest of urban America.

Interior of St. Patrick's Cathedral at the occasion of the Grand Fair of the Roman Catholic Churches
of New York City, 1878. From *Frank Leslie's Illustrated Newspaper*. Museum of the City of New York,
The J. Clarence Davies Collection.

THE IRISH BEAUTY.

Published by J.Dorival.52 Ann St N.Y.

142.

(*Above*) "Be Gorrah." (*Opposite*) *Irish Beauty*. Colored lithographs.
Two assessments of the "typical" Irish immigrant.

Irish silver miners at the Comstock Lode in Nevada. These miners look fairly nonchalant
having just discovered one of the largest silver strikes in the country.

Gold panners near Rockerville, Dakota Territory, 1889.
Gold miners covered the western territories from Montana to California.

A CLOSER LOOK:
JOHN BOYLE O'REILLY
Edited with permission of Thomas J. O'Gorman

As a member of the Irish Republican Brotherhood, John Boyle O'Reilly (1844-1890) was arrested and tried on a charge of high treason. His death sentence was commuted to deportation to Australia from which he launched a daring escape.

O'Reilly found quick success in the U.S. In 1870, he obtained a position on the staff of the Boston newspaper, *The Pilot*. There, his poetic observations received wide acclaim.

Late nineteenth-century Boston was alive with the ethos of America's great and glorious past. The power of such dramatic history very much intrigued the poetic imagination of John Boyle O'Reilly and would often become the subject of his verse.

O'Reilly's poetic verse of itself brought a new insight into the dynamic of assimilation for the Irish of America. Very often the subject of O'Reilly's verse had its imagery in the glorious, romantic heroics of America's finest moments or its highest political ideals. He really believed that America was the land of the free. His words advertised that insight to many who were not sure if this was indeed a nation in which to put their trust. O'Reilly would always remain an Irish patriot, but he was transfixed by the opportunity to discover a broader patriotism within the detail and duties of American life.

O'Reilly became enraged by the squalid and wretched conditions which black men, women, and children were forced to endure. While in the American South, he discovered many cruel and inhuman conditions. "If ever the color question comes up again, as long as I live," he said, "I shall be counted in with the black men." His personal experience with freedom, and the lack of it, had burrowed egalitarianism deeply within him.

A man full of health and spirit, O'Reilly's death (from ingesting an improperly prepared sleeping potion) came as a great shock to his friends and admirers, as well as to the legions of his fellow Irishmen to whom his heart was pledged. He remained at the time of his death an unpardoned traitor against the British government. He gloried in this fact. *The New York Times* said: "Mr. O'Reilly was best known for his ardent interest and activity in every cause that related to his native land, but he will longer be remembered for his graceful and spirited poems and for the romantic experiences of his early life."

John Boyle O'Reilly's memory is written still on the hearts and character of the Boston Irish he loved so well. More than a century after his death, his shadow continues to fall with a dashing, gentlemanly stride across the cobbles of the North End or the patriot soil of Bunker Hill in his own beloved Charlestown. From the careful refinements of Brookline to the fog-bound, clapboard

homes of Hull, he is woven into the folklore and consciousness of Beantown life, like a bowl of chowder or Fourth of July fireworks on the Esplanade.

In the lush greenwood of Holyhood Cemetery on the edge of Brookline, John Boyle O'Reilly rests amid the successful, mani-cured Irish of 1 th-century Boston; his monument, a monolithic Irish boulder from the sacred soil of Dowth Castle, County Meath—the exiled land of his boyhood—carried in tribute to his final, Fenian resting place.

(Above) Steam shovel at Hanging Rock, Echo Canyon, 1869, during construction of the Union Pacific Railroad.

(Left) Union Pacific pay car at Blue Creek, Utah, spring 1869.

Driving the golden spike at Promontory, Utah, May 10, 1869.
The Irish were the principle source of labor in building
the transcontinental railroad that linked East and West in 1869.

Varina Howell Davis was the daughter of an Irishman who according to legend fled
from Ireland after killing a man, then fled from Virginia after another fatal duel, then fled south.
She then became the First Lady of the Confederacy.

Margaret Mary Healy Murphy standing next to her husband,
John Bernard Murphy, a rancher in San Patricio County, Texas, late 1870s.

(Top) Margaret Reese and Pat Burke playing "Bottle Horsies" at their grandfather's ranch in Live Oak County, Texas.

(Left) Oscar Fagan at the Fagan home in Texas, built 1868.

Margaret Hefferman Hardy Borland, c. 1872, the first woman to lead a trail drive.
She died in Kansas of trail fever, at the end of the line.

A CLOSER LOOK:
IN-DEPTH APPROACH

John Philip Holland was born in County Clare in 1841. Poor eyesight prevented him from pursuing a seafaring career, like his father. He joined the Christian Brothers, and taught in several of their schools. Dispensed from his vows in 1872, he emigrated to the United States, where he found work as a schoolteacher in Patterson, New Jersey. After these experiences, his mind turned again to the sea—or, rather, to travel beneath its surface.

Largely self-taught as an engineer, Holland spent years experimenting with designs for a "submarine vessel," the ultimate weapon of that period, sought by governments and their scientific advisers throughout the world. Much of Holland's early backing came from Irish friends, particularly in Nationalist circles. John Devoy, the exiled Fenian leader, raised several hundred thousand dollars in the hope of securing a "Fenian Ram" that could be used against the British fleet. Forming his own naval engineering company in 1895, Holland secured contracts from the U.S. Navy, and by 1900 had produced a craft that met their standards. Within a few years, the practical entrepreneur was also selling his "undersea boats" to the once-loathed Royal Navy.

John Philip Holland died in Newark, New Jersey, in August 1914, a few days after the outbreak of the First World War. The one-time Christian Brother had become the "Father of the Submarine," and his creation was about to become the war's most formidable instrument of destruction.

(Below) **John Holland, second from right, and his backers.**

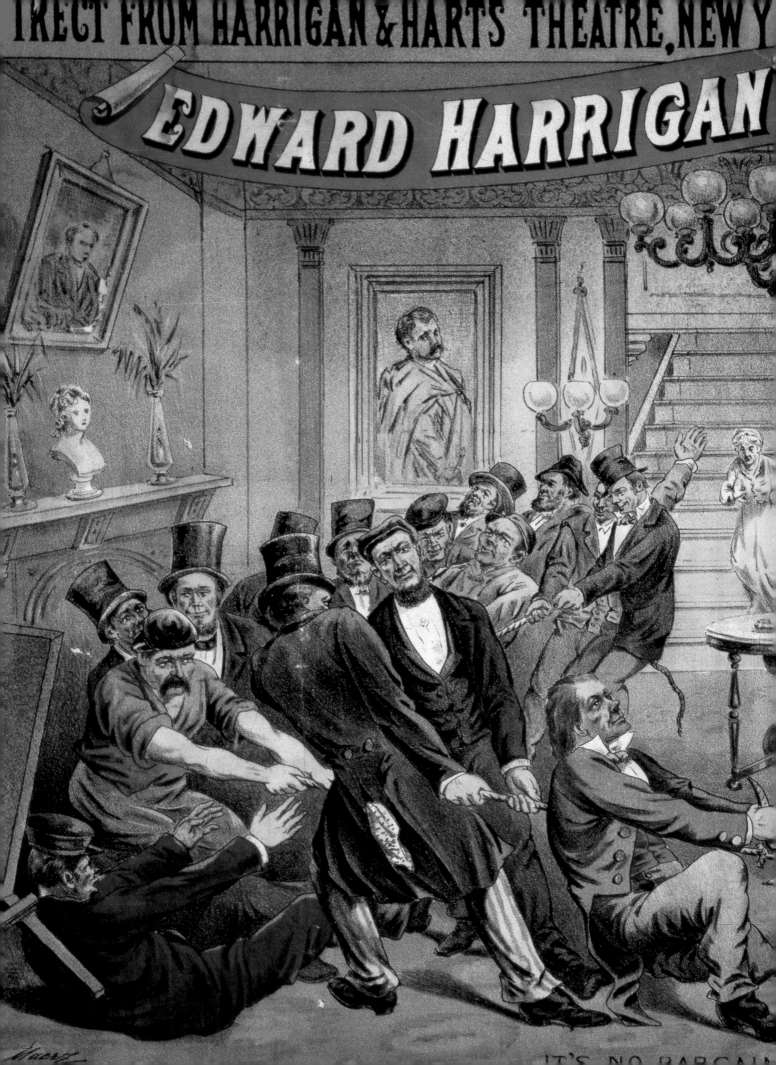

SQUATTER SOVEREIGNTY,

"ROUT THE GOAT."

THE IRISH LEARN HOW TO COPE WITH AMERICA (1890–1920)

Ellis Island opened in 1892, to replace the old Castle Garden facility that had processed so many Irish immigrants since the 1850s. The first person to be admitted at the gateway to America was a young Irish girl. But it would be "new" immigrants, from southern and eastern Europe, who would predominate on the island during the next three decades. When these Italians, Slavs, and Russian Jews came ashore in New York, they might well have imagined that they had arrived in Dublin instead. Irishmen patrolled the streets, put out the fires, staffed the offices, and collected taxes. Irish women taught in the schools, nursed in the hospitals, cooked in the restaurants, and presided behind the shop counters. If the newcomers sought a glimpse of American sports they found that the Irish were the boxing and baseball heroes, as well as providing a wide array of celebrities and "characters." Should the immigrant try for a taste of American popular culture, he might well encounter Irish singers, dancers, musicians, actors, humorists, and journalists filling up the stage and the press with Celtic wit, art, and sentiment.

America had learned how to cope with the Irish by concentrating on their positive contributions to the country and putting up with their more distressing traits. Now the Irish were learning how to cope with life in America—essentially by taking over major segments of it and shaping it to suit their own needs, while giving it an Irish stamp in the process. Their achievements ranged from City Hall to the music hall.

(Previous spread) "It's No Bargain Without the Goat." Harrigan and Hart advertising poster. Museum of the City of New York. Harrigan and Hart were the turn-of-the-century's most prolific showmen.

(Opposite) George M. Cohan was the creator of the modern musical comedy in which a plot replaces the earlier practice of unconnected review sketches strung together.

The wedding of Ellen L. Maher and Michael A. McCormick in Newport, Rhode Island, 1896.

THE IRISH: "AMERICA'S POLITICAL CLASS"

The story of how "politics" became virtually synonymous with "Irish" in the United States begins with the founding of the Democratic Party headquarters in New York City just after the Revolutionary War. Although Tammany Hall welcomed Irish immigrants and aided them in becoming citizen-voters, they played only a subordinate role in the Party, as loyal "foot soldiers," until the Civil War period—the time of the Tweed Ring.

William M. Tweed was the first in the line of Tammany "bosses" who presided over New York as it grew into an international center of commerce, culture, and political power. Himself of Scottish descent, Boss Tweed had Irishmen—Richard Connolly, the comptroller, and Peter Sweeny, the city chamberlain—as his principal collaborators, and shared the spoils of office with a multitude of "faithful Hibernians" in the party ranks during his ascendency, from the end of the Civil War until 1871. Nevertheless, when the blatant fraud and corruption of the Tweed Ring finally roused an outcry for reform, it was an alliance between the old

New York "elite" and insurgent Irish Catholics that finally drove its members from office. The evidence of colossal thefts from the public treasury was uncovered by a journalist named Matthew O'Rourke. Tweed was prosecuted by Charles O'Connor (later the first Irish Catholic nominated for the presidency). And John Kelly, who was married to a niece of New York's Cardinal McCloskey, succeeded Tweed, becoming the first Irish Catholic Tammany boss. Tammany soon arranged the election of New York's first Irish Catholic mayor, William R. Grace, an immigrant cabin boy who had made his fortune through the Grace Shipping Line.

Annie Moore, a native of Ireland, was the first immigrant to pass through the new reception facility on Ellis Island in 1892. Here she is shown a few years later with her own daughter.

It was said of "Honest John" Kelly, who controlled New York politics from 1872 to 1886, that "he found Tammany a horde and left it an army." He recognized the sprawling party network, which Tweed had neglected during his looting of the city, and created the orderly apparatus upon which his successors' authority rested. The structure of every major party organization in every city in the United States is still essentially patterned after Kelly's Tammany Hall. Honest John, the largely self-taught son of a grocer from County Tyrone, was

Turn-of-the-century police raid. Both the enforcers and the breakers of the law in this period were often Irish Americans.

Dance at Tammany
Hall headquarters of
the New York
Democratic Party, 1910.
The Irish were the
political leaders of New
York at this period.

a "quiet, sober, pious man" who had once aspired to the priesthood. As the only Catholic among the 241 members of the United States Congress, he had been a bold defender of the Church against nativist attacks, and "the champion of the Irish on Capitol Hill." In his reconstruction of Tammany he was clearly influenced by the Church's sense of hierarchy and authority and its capacity for maintaining institutional discipline. The system was paternalistic. Its leaders, who had fought their way up from the city's masses, "spoke the language of the poor," and their granting of favors in return for votes was more acceptable to most immigrants than the "impersonal charity" offered by Tammany opponents. "If a family is burned out," said George Washington Plunkitt, one of Kelly's district leaders, "I don't ask whether they are Republicans or Democrats . . . I just get quarters for them, buy clothes for them if their clothes were burned up, and fix them up 'til they get things running again. It's philanthropy, but it's politics, too—mighty good politics. Who can tell how many votes one of these fires brings me?" The same durable politician (he was "on the New York scene" until 1924) described Honest John's organization as "a great big machine with every part adjusted delicately to do its own particular work, It runs so smooth that you wouldn't think it was a complicated affair, but it is." Kelly was able to win elections by dispensing favors to the voters and party workers, thereby gaining more public offices to dispense more favors. This self-perpetuating system was, it has been noted by political scientists, "a smaller and more intimate precursor of the New Deal." And Franklin D. Roosevelt, the creator of the New Deal, was, of course, a New York politician whose first political steps were taken under the patronage of Tammany.

Under Kelly and his heirs, Richard Croker (boss from 1886 until he retired to a castle in his native Ireland in 1901) and Charles F. Murphy (who presided in the Hall until his death in 1924), New York became the

James Farley with FDR and Louis Howe. Farley served as chairman of the Democratic Party and was a leading figure in national politics during Roosevelt's administration in which he served as Postmaster-General.

(Above) Women factory workers in New England were called "fair unveiled Nuns of Industry" by poet John Greenleaf Whittier.

(Right) These mill-workers in Lynn, Massachusetts, 1895, represent the positive and forward-looking spirit among Irish-American workers stimulated by the rising power of labor unions in which they played such a formative role. Photographs by Frances Benjamin Johnston.

John Fitzgerald, popularly known as "Honey Fitz," was mayor of Boston and an exponent of "machine politics." Here he is shown laying the cornerstone for the High School of Practical Arts in Boston in 1912.

first great city to be ruled by men of the people, not in a brief revolutionary moment, but in a consistent pattern of power. In *Beyond the Melting Pot,* Daniel P. Moynihan and Nathan Glazer have affirmed that the Irish role was "creative, not imitative." The system they established in New York (and which was duplicated in many other cities) drew upon their experience in their homeland, with its flexible political proprieties and tradition of informal, "popular" government undercutting the formal regime. To this they had added the experience of organizing mass political movements learned in the Ireland of Daniel O'Connell. Men like the cold, distant Charles Murphy, whom even his closest associates addressed as "Mister Murphy," and Hugh McLaughlin, who ruled the Brooklyn Democrats from 1862 to 1903, were far from the "genial Irishman" of American folklore. They were firm, efficient administrators of a political system in which deference and reliability received their due reward. The Irish-American boss perceived himself not as a tyrant, but as an expediter, working through a web of local bosses to aid "the people," who sustained his party in power. "Why must there be a boss," a reformer once asked Croker, "when we've got a mayor, and a council, and a . . ." "That's why," interrupted Croker. "It's because there's a mayor, *and* a council, *and* a hundred other men to deal with." The boss, in his view, was not a tyrant, but an imposer of order upon the complexities of modern urban bureaucracy.

The Tammany model was replicated, with minor variations, in Boston and Chicago, Philadelphia and Kansas City, and dozens of other towns, large and small. It endured in many places long after it faded away in its birthplace, following Murphy's death. There were already critics of "municipal corruption" among the Progressives of the 1890s. Mayor John Fitzgerald of Boston mocked these "good government" advocates as "goo-goos," defying reformers and Brahmins alike. Once the Irish had mastered the arts of paternalism and patronage in the new urban setting, it would take more than genteel expostulation to dislodge them. As one commentator put it, the Irish had become "America's political class."

IDOLS OF THE CROWD

Just as those who considered themselves the natural rulers of America conceded the role of managing the cities to the Irish, so they surrendered the status of popular hero to the sons (and, occasionally, the daughters) of Erin. By the end of the nineteenth century, the White Anglo-Saxon Protestant elite no longer generated the kind of mass appeal that provided the idols of the crowd. The celebrities of the new era, often dismissed by the

The Knights of the Red Branch, an Irish-American fraternal organization based in San Francisco, are pictured outside of their temporary hall in the aftermath of the earthquake of 1906. Many of the members had strong Fenian links including ties to the Irish community in Australia.

John L. Sullivan, Idol of the American Crowd and subsequent vaudeville performer and temperance lecturer.

"genteel element" as violent or vulgar, were increasingly drawn from the ranks of the Irish immigrant. No sport, for instance, was more violent and vulgar, or more popular, than boxing, and the rise of the Irish to ascendency in this field illustrates this aspect of their immigrant experience.

No one needed to teach the Irish how to fight; it was the English, however, who taught them the art of boxing. They took to it readily (unlike other aspects of the British civilizing mission), and, by the late eighteenth century, Irishmen like Pat Corcoran dominated the prize ring.

John L. Sullivan, Champion Pugilist of the World. Lithograph poster. Currier & Ives, 1882. The "Boston Strong Boy," a world-wide celebrity as much for his boasting as his boxing, was ultimately defeated by "Gentleman Jim Corbett."

Dan Donnelly, who bested a string of English champions in the early 1800s, became a legend and an inspiration to generations of Irish pugilists on both sides of the Atlantic. In his brief, heavy-drinking, free-spending career, he offered a dramatic, if unedifying role model to those young immigrants who brawled their way into celebrity during the post-Famine years.

Fighters like Mike McCool and Joe Coburn came "off the boat" in the 1840s to punch their way to prominence in America, and Cork-born James Ambrose (fighting as "Yank Sullivan") was bare-knuckle champion of the United States until 1853, when he was defeated by John Morrissey, who had arrived from Tipperary as a child and perfected his skills as a teenage thug on the mean streets of New York. Unlike many boxers, "Old Smoke" Morrissey (nicknamed for a brawl in which he kept on punching even when his clothes caught fire) was a shrewd manager of his own earnings. He eventually became owner of a fashionable casino in Saratoga Springs and a member of Congress. Yet most Americans of "the better sort" drew no distinction between the immigrant success story of Morrissey and the fate of Yank Sullivan, who died under mysterious circumstances in a California jail cell. In the view of the genteel element, pugilism, gambling, and politics were the natural habitat of the drinking, fighting, disreputable Irish, whom they continued to hold in low esteem.

The general image, and acceptance, of the Irish in America was changing in the post–Civil War years, as John Lawrence Sullivan was growing to manhood, and the "Boston Strong Boy" would play a crucial role in changing the status of boxing in the country as well. Born in 1858, the son of an immigrant, he evaded his mother's plan that he should study for the priesthood, and became a plumber's apprentice. His size, strength, and flair for self-promotion soon launched him on the more spectacular career of prize-fighter, ultimately victorious in two hundred bouts. In 1882 Sullivan defeated Paddy Ryan to become the heavyweight champion of the United States.

Although "the Great John L." would fight other bare-knuckle bouts (notably his epic seventy-five-round contest with Jake Kilrane in1889), he favored the replacement of the old London Prize Ring standards, which gave virtual free rein to mayhem, by the newly developed Marquis of Queensberry Rules, with their fixed-length rounds, establishment of ring conditions, introduction of padded gloves, and prohibition of "unsports-manlike" tactics. His endorsement of these principles, especially after winning under the old semibarbarous rules, did much to secure recognition for boxing as a sport.

During the ten years of his reign, Sullivan became a national, rather than merely an Irish-American, hero. Traveling to the British Isles and Australia to defend his title, he secured international renown, like Buffalo Bill, as a larger-than-life New World folk figure. Always outspoken and "natural" (seeking the family cottage in Ireland, he blurted, "I guess the old man was a good judge, to get out of here!"), Sullivan was also a boozer and a brag-gart, whose contempt for his adversaries was loudly proclaimed. Nevertheless, when "Gentleman Jim" Corbett laid him low in 1892, he accepted his defeat with surprising good grace. Sullivan never fought again, but renewed his popularity by playing himself in stage shows and as a temperance lecturer, denouncing his former bad habits. When he died in

1918, thousands attended the funeral of the first boxer to become not only an ethnic, but a national, legend.

At the beginning of the twentieth century, the Irish still dominated the prize ring in the United States. But the more recent immigrants, and the now-established descendants of earlier "exiles," were growing uncomfortable with the stereotype of the "pugnacious Celt." As early as 1905, the Ancient Order of Hibernians was deploring the growing custom of "criminals and boxers" adopting Irish names.

Despite the distress of the upwardly mobile Irish, enough working-class youths still sought fame and fortune through fisticuffs to perpetuate a dynasty of champions named Fitzsimmons, O'Brien, Dillon, and O'Dowd. What amounted to the final round of the Irish dominance of American boxing did not come until the 1920s, when the championship held by Jack Dempsey was captured by Gene Tunney, who successfully defended it against the "Mauler's" comeback attempt in 1927.

Baseball, in this, its formative period, was another venue for Irish–American popular heroes. Although it did not permit the kind of dominance offered by boxing, the "national pastime" created many stars of the season, and at least two enduring "legends"—John McGraw and Connie Mack (Cornelius McGillicuddy), whose managerial talents and rivalries helped reinforce the game's popularity.

John McGraw, manager of one of the most prominent baseball teams in the opening years of the 20th century.

Connie Mack
(Cornelius
McGillicuddy), the
great rival of
John McGraw, is
pictured with his
players.

In addition to the sporting life, the general stream of celebrity provided a flow of eccentrics and "people in the news" in the days when newspapers and magazines had the field of sensationalism all to themselves. Indeed, Nellie Bly (Elizabeth Cochran) crossed the line between reporting and personal notoriety by infiltrating prisons, madhouses, and other such "unknown" institutions and then writing exposés on conditions therein. The most famous escapade was nothing less than a high-speed trip around the world in which she beat the record set by Jules Verne's *80 Days*.

Margaret Tobin Brown, a hard-luck immigrant's daughter from Colorado, married a more fortunate gold miner, and became the classic nouveau riche American, building a lavishly furnished mansion in Denver, laughing off the snubs of the gentry, and making a match for her young sister with a German nobleman. Her greatest fame was achieved in 1912, when, proclaiming herself the "Unsinkable Molly Brown," she raised the spirits and aided the survival of the women and children who escaped the sinking of the *Titanic*.

Another goldminer's daughter, Evelyn Walsh McLean, also won celebrity for her extravagance, most notably through the acquisition of the Hope Diamond, the fabulous and ill-starred gem so beloved of tabloid reporters.

Also among diamond fanciers, though on a more practical scale, was James Buchanan Brady, the dandy and man-about-town whose opulent array included personal jewelry that earned him the sobriquet "Diamond Jim."

In stark contrast to these gaudy folk was Mary Elizabeth Lease, the "Queen of the Populists," whose exhortation to Kansas farmers to "raise

The parlor of Molly
Brown's home in
Denver. Her ostenta-
tious nouveau riche
style was the object of
derision by members
of the local gentry.

less wheat and more hell" endeared her to working-class reformers of the
1890s. She had honed her rhetorical skills by accompanying her father to
Irish nationalist meetings among the midwestern Fenians.

Joining her among vocal opponents of
the plutocracy was the Irish-born Mary
Jones, whose activity in labor organizing
and the promotion of "radical causes"
kept her to the fore over the decades.
By the time of her death at the age of
one hundred, she was revered by the
American Left as "Mother Jones."

Diamond Jim Brady at the races. When not
lording it over banquet tables or escorting
actresses like Lillian Russell about town, Brady
occupied his time between the race course
and questionable financial dealings.

Mary Harris Jones, Irish immigrant and Grand Old Lady of the American Labor Movement. Her 100 years spanned the rise of trade unionism in the U.S. and encompassed the period of the greatest Irish influence in the movement.

Whether fighting for fame, fortune, or a cause, the Irish had learned how to win a following in America.

CULTURE SHIFT

The immigrants of the Famine era brought with them the fragments of their native culture. Some of these, such as their language, they soon discarded. Others, like music and dance, they preserved (or revived, as with the traditional sports promoted by the Gaelic Athletic Association in the 1890s).

But, for the most part, the Irish adapted themselves to the prevailing popular culture. Indeed, they found their own niche in the performing arts, where four generations of actors named Tyrone Power, the actress Ada Rehan, and the tragedian James O'Neill (whose personal tragedy was imaged by his son, Eugene, in *Long Day's Journey into Night*), and dozens of others made "Irish" and "stage" almost synonymous at the turn of the century.

American popular music also took on an Irish flavor. The "reviews" of Harrigan and Hart gave way to the fully plotted musical comedies created by George M. Cohan. The Dublin-born Victor Herbert's operettas rivaled those of continental composers in popularity. Song-and-dance men like Pat Rooney delighted vaudeville theater audiences, while John McCormack's magnificent tenor voice thrilled the more upscale patrons of the opera house (though he remained ready to perform the sentimental ballads of Ireland in America).

The popular press provided an alternate outlet for Irish exuberance. In the pages of mass circulation dailies and lurid weeklies, the verbally adroit sons

Miss Ada Rehan. Lithograph poster. David Allen & Sons, c. 1887.
Museum of the City of New York. Ada Rehan, prominent Irish-American
actress, is seen here in *The Taming of the Shrew*.

(Left) James O'Neill, the celebrated Irish-American actor, and father of Eugene O'Neill.

(Right) Eugene O'Neill and his family in the garden of their home.

and grandsons of "tempest-tossed refugees" were secure enough in their own identity as "Yanks" to chronicle the crimes, follies, and vices of the exotic folk who were now arriving from overseas. A few journalists retained a distinct ethnic insight, however, when it came to covering sports or crime (where the "cops and robbers" might still both be Irish).

At the point where journalism, humor, and the art of the popular essay intersected, the Chicago writer Finley Peter Dunne occupied a special place. His columns (later published in book form) recounting the opinions of "Mr. Dooley," were set in an Irish-American saloon and were redolent of urban dialect. Their wit and wisdom nevertheless transcended mere Irish comic dialogue and brought a sharp satiric focus on the personalities and issues of the day.

A different approach to "becoming American" was taken by the founders of the American Irish Historical Society. Instead of merging into the American mainstream through the shared laughter and tears of popular culture, the business and professional men who established this organization in 1897 sought to co-opt American history for the Irish by

A scene from *Long Day's Journey into Night*, Eugene O'Neill's vision of a father and son in conflict.

Robert Spencer. *On the Canal, New Hope.* 1916. Oil on canvas. The Detroit Institute of Arts, gift of Miss Julia E. Peck. A glimpse of a less genteel Irish-American environment in which some of the less mobile of the population still found themselves.

(Above) **Second- and third-generation Irish Americans, c. 1910, Newport, Rhode Island.**

(Opposite) Mullen's Alley, c. 1890. **Photograph: Jacob A. Riis Collection, Museum of the City of New York.**

documenting and publicizing the fact that the Irish had been in the country in significant numbers since colonial days. One of several filiopietistic ethnic historical groups set up at the same period, it sprang directly from anti-Catholic riots in Boston during the mid 1890s. These outbursts, generated by the American Protective Association, a latter-day nativist organization, resulted from an attempt to lump the Irish in with the newer "foreigners" who seemed to be overrunning America. The "lace curtain" and "assimilated" character of the AIHS is reflected in its structural imitation of such long-established bodies as the Massachusetts Historical Society as well as its emphasis on the pre-Famine period of Irish-American history. The articles in its *Journal* (written by gentlemen amateur historians), its field days, and historical markers all reveal a tendency to claim more for the Irish role in nation-building than strict accuracy might justify, and at the same time, an earnest desire to be accepted as 100 percent American. By the early 1920s, the society was runing out of steam, and becoming little more than a social club. But by that time, the Irish had found other ways to confirm their place in America.

A CLOSER LOOK:
FATHER AND SON

During the century between the end of the Napoleonic Wars and the outbreak of the First World War, two generations of an Irish immigrant family produced the leading theoreticians of military and naval tactics. The Mahans, father and son, shaped the thinking of generals and admirals, as well as stimulated America's imperial vision.

Denis Hart Mahan was the son of immigrants who exchanged the revolutionary tumult of 1790's Ireland for the stability and opportunity of Virginia. His parents had both the substance and the political influence to get Denis an appointment to the recently created United States Military Academy, from which he graduated, with distinction, in 1817. So impressed were his superiors with young Lieutenant Mahan's abilities that they sent him to France for advanced study. On his return, he was appointed to the teaching staff at West Point, where he remained for some forty years, much of that time as Dean of Faculty. "Professor Mahan," as he was universally known, structured the curriculum, and guided the thinking that underlay American military policy down to the early years of the Civil War. An admirer of Bonaparte, he imparted his concept of Napoleonic tactics to the cadets who became Union and Confederate generals.

Although raised on the West Point campus, the professor's son, Alfred Thayer Mahan, chose to attend Annapolis. After coastal blockade duties during the Civil War, he spent two decades of uneventful cruising in the peacetime navy. Mahan put those years to good use, however, in study and reflection on history. In 1886, Captain Mahan delivered a series of lectures at the Naval War College that won him the presidency of that institution, and, when published, secured his fame. *The Influence of Seapower Upon History* demonstrated the vital role that control of the world's sea lanes would have upon the geopolitics of the new age of imperialism. Through this, and subsequent volumes of historical and theoretical analysis, Mahan became not only the "Prophet of Navalism," but a major force in American expansionism. By the time of his death in 1914, the United States had "a Navy second to none," and ranked as a world power.

View of the United States Military Academy from the Hudson R

A St. Louis, Missouri, street scene, c. 1910. Photograph by Dick Lemen.

Playground in Poverty Gap–Alley Gang preserves, c. 1890. Photograph by Jacob Riis.

(*Left*) Children poised outside O'Keeffe's store near Boston, c. 1910.

(*Below*) Interior of a specialty teas and coffee emporium.

A working man's tavern, c. 1907.

John Sloan. *McSorley's Bar.* 1912. Oil on canvas. 26 x 32 in. Detroit Institute of Arts, Founders Society Purchase.

A newsgirl in a fancy hat in 1896 New York City.

Policeman with foundling, New York City. Photograph by Lewis Hine.

The Ladies Auxiliary of the Ancient Order of Hibernians, Kilkenny, Minnesota, c. 1910.

The Ancient Order of Hibernians, Kilkenny, Minnesota, c. 1910–15.

THE VANISHING IRISH
(1920–1960)

During the four decades between the end of World War I and the preliminaries of the Vietnam War, the United States underwent profound, convulsive changes. During the same period, the Irish in America, once so highly visible, seemed to fade from view, until they were described, like the American Indians, as "vanishing" from the national scene. This comparative invisibility was not simply America's collective attention being distracted by the dramatic occurrences of the day. The Irish, in fact, were undergoing their own set of changes. The culmination of Ireland's struggle for independence and the consequent decline of Irish nationalism as a unifying force in the transatlantic diaspora, was followed by a sharp decline in immigration, which diminished the "Irishness" of the community in the United States. Shifting patterns of social and economic assimilation, particularly after World War II, accelerated the loss of identity. And, ironically, the very triumph of the 1960 election, in which an Irish Catholic won the presidency, marked the end of an Irish political class that was distinct from the broad national stream of American politics.

FREE STATE: CLOSED DOOR

There have always been Irish Americans, but Irish America came to existence during the Famine era and it was, in essence, the transatlantic

(Previous spread) **A gala reception following a Pablo Casals Concert at the White House shortly after the election of John Fitzgerald Kennedy.**

(Opposite) **Mark Twain's Huckleberry Finn, here portrayed by actor Mickey Rooney, was an embodiment of many Irish virtues and vices as perceived by 19th-century Anglo-Americans. He was also the quintessential American boy.**

This scene from the film *Michael Collins* depicts the Proclamation of the Irish Republic at the beginning of the 1916 Easter Rebellion.

sanctuary and supply depot of Ireland's nationalist political movements. Irish America supplied moral, financial, and—at times—military commitments. Although critics in the United States charged that all Irish Americans were obsessed with Ireland, neglecting their patriotic obligations to their new country, most Irish Americans were merely nominal, sentimental supporters of Irish nationalism, and many lost interest in the old country as soon as they set foot in the new. For the hard core who constituted Irish America, however, the winning of Ireland's freedom remained a priority, from the days of the Young Irelanders and the Fenians onward.

During the 1880s, Ireland swung back to the nonviolent line of nationalism formerly promoted by Daniel O'Connell. The Land League, with its advocacy of tenant farmers' rights, and the Home Rule movement, which sought an autonomous Irish parliament within the structure of the United Kingdom, captured a majority of nationalists in Ireland, and in Irish America. Charles Stewart Parnell, the Home Rule leader, toured the United States, and was even given the honor of addressing the House of Representatives (in recognition of his status as the grandson of the naval hero Commodore Charles Stewart, and of the importance of the Irish-American vote).

Although Home Rule languished after Parnell's death in 1891, Irish America remained focused on Ireland. Cultural nationalists, like the author/educator Patrick Pearse, solicited contributions for their projects from well-to-do Irish Americans, and James Connolly, who had helped introduce both Marxian socialism and the Trade Union movement in Ireland, spent several years in the United States at the turn of the century promoting a Socialist-Revolutionary concept of the nationalist cause.

A neo-Fenian resurgence in the years leading up to the First World War culminated in the "Easter Rebellion" of 1916, in which Pearse, Connolly, and their followers raised the Irish nationalist tricolor over Dublin's principal buildings and proclaimed the independence of Ireland. Irish America had supported the activities that led up to this insurrection, and looked on with awe and sympathy as the rebels made their "blood sacrifice" and succumbed to the might of the British Empire, after a week of street battles. While the other leaders were quickly executed, a team of Irish-American lawyers was able to save the life of the New York–born rebel commandant, Eamon De Valera (son of an Irish mother and a Spanish father), by arguing

Eamon DeValera (pictured here with his three sons) was an American-born hero of the Irish national struggle culminating in the establishment of the Irish Free State in 1921. His opposition to what he regarded as compromise led to a civil war in Ireland.

Leader of the Irish Free State Eamon DeValera chats with Cardinal Hayes of New York during the Eucharistic Congress in Dublin in 1932.

that he still enjoyed the protection of United States citizenship.

Both Ireland and Irish America remained in a state of agitation in the aftermath of the Easter Rebellion, and early in 1919 a self-proclaimed national legislature reasserted Irish independence, launching a bloody guerrilla war that raged on into 1921. De Valera, now president of the Dail Eireann (as the Irish legislature was formally called) toured the United States to rally the enthusiasts, promote the sale of Irish Republican bonds, and propagandize among non–Irish Americans who were potential sympathizers with this anticolonial struggle. In 1920 the British set up a self-governing entity, "Northern Ireland," in the six northeastern counties, with an overall Protestant majority population, and in the following year initiated a cease-fire and peace talks with the nationalist leadership. The result, which came into being in 1922, was the Irish Free State.

Comprising the twenty-six remaining counties (overwhelmingly Catholic in population), the Free State represented a compromise by the nationalist leaders who signed the Anglo-Irish Treaty of 1921 accepting the partition of Ireland. De Valera and the "Anti-Treaty" faction rejected the idea of partition and the dominion status within the Empire Commonwealth which the Free State government accepted while dropping the name of "Republic." The irreconcilable Republicans launched an armed rebellion of their own, but after a brief civil war, the Free State emerged as the new regime in Ireland.

Most Irish Americans accepted the Free State as the fulfillment of their hereditary aspirations for an independent Ireland. A minority continued to cling doggedly to the dream of a thirty-two-county united Ireland. They were not even appeased by the replacement of the "Irish Free State" by "Eire" in 1937, or the end of the last ties with Britain in 1949, when the Republic of Ireland was formally proclaimed in Dublin.

Despite this residual dissatisfaction, Irish America virtually ceased to exist when the Free State was established in 1922. With Ireland free at last, Americans of Irish birth or descent could turn their attention fully to "getting on" with life "over here."

The birth of the Irish Free State coincided almost exactly with the virtual closing of America's door to immigration. Restrictions imposed in 1925 sharply limited, and nearly eliminated, access to a country that had decided it already had too many foreigners. While the Irish were no longer the prime target of xenophobia, their right to settle in America was placed under quota.

Long before the limitations imposed by the United States Congress, however, the crises in Ireland that had forced such massive movement across the Atlantic in former days had eased, and the number of immigrants entering the United States had naturally diminished over several decades.

During the first decade of the twentieth century, little more than thirty

The long corridor at Ellis Island that led Irish immigrants to residences in the United States was blocked by the revised immigration laws of the 1920s.

163

thousand Irish immigrants a year entered the country, and the average declined to about twenty thousand a year thereafter, until the lowered quota reduced the annual intake to one thousand or less during the 1930s, a figure which only crept up to, and then slightly over, the five thousand per year level during Ireland's economic doldrums in the 1950s.

The decline in Irish immigration to the United States deprived the existing Irish community of the "fresh blood" that would have preserved its vitality. With so few arriving who could, in effect, "update" the Irish in America on the changing nature of Irish life, the aging population of Irish-born Americans would, during the period between 1920 and 1960, exhibit an increasingly sentimental and outdated view of Ireland. Moreover, as the older generation gradually died off, their American-born children and grandchildren would, inevitably, become "Americanized." With the age-old "Irish Question" seemingly resolved to the satisfaction of all but a handful of antipartition crusaders, the incentive to dwell upon the problems of a small, distant island was likewise diminished.

Irish immigrants, Boston, 1921.

The melting pot awaited.

NEW JOBS,
NEW NEIGHBORHOODS

Three Irish-American novelists of the 1920s and 1930s offer as much insight into the evolution of the immigrant as do a set of statistics. F. Scott Fitzgerald, born in the Irish enclave of St. Paul, Minnesota, John O'Hara, from western Pennsylvania, and James T. Farrell, a product of Chicago's Irish stronghold, each represented an aspect of the shifting social, economic, and cultural identity of this period.

F. Scott Fitzgerald and his family, c. 1925.

Fitzgerald's family, while certainly not among the small group of Irish who had made it to "the top" in America, was sufficiently well-to-do to provide him with the money and upbringing to facilitate his entrance into Princeton, from which his personal charm and talents soon carried him into a spectacularly successful (at least in its early stages) career as a novelist and short-story writer. Fitzgerald's writing, his characters—his whole literary and personal style—reflect the attitude of the thoroughly assimilated Irish American, who considers himself and his work purely American. Some critics might point to Fitzgerald's drinking, his recklessness with money, and his tendency toward social climbing as negative manifestations of his Irish heritage, but these flaws are hardly exclusive to the Irish.

John O'Hara's social insecurity, on the other hand, is evident throughout his career. The son of a physician, O'Hara was a popular writer who was far more adept at holding on to his earnings than Fitzgerald. He was frustrated by his provincial middle-class origins and seems to have longed for acceptance by the Ivy League elite, imitating their dress and lifestyle and chronicling their doings with a mixture of resentment and envy. Whereas Fitzgerald virtually ignored the Irish, O'Hara introduced a number of

John O'Hara.

repulsive Irish-American characters in his novels and stories. Far from being at ease in his "Americanness," O'Hara was acutely conscious of his origins, sensing that they would keep him from being admitted to "the best society," and revealed his bitterness over the "albatross of ethnicity" that would always deny him admission to that charmed circle.

James T. Farrell had no bourgeois pretensions or illusions. The setting of his *Studs Lonigan* trilogy is the working-class Irish community in Chicago, and his many subsequent (although far less critically acclaimed) novels reflect a persistent consciousness and realism about origin and identity. Some of his protagonists sink into petty crime or alcoholic despair. These people are not members of a degraded underclass. They have families, employment, even aspirations of self-improvement. Their greatest disadvantage is an intellectual deprivation, imposed upon them by the Catholic clergy, which severs ties with their past while isolating them from the cultural life of 1920's America, declared by the priests to be full of threats to the Faith.

Irish-American parochialism (both literal and figurative) might be rejected or lamented by writers, but it remained a socioeconomic fact of life through the 1920s and 1930s. As long as descendants of the immigrants remained in the settings created by their predecessors, they stayed a distinct community despite the fading of the nationalist cause and the drying-up of the immigrant flow.

The Irish had been in the forefront of the struggle between labor and management ever since the Molly Maguire violence in the Pennsylvania coalfields after the Civil War. They had taken the lead in organizing unions and had achieved a solid position in a wide variety of skilled trades during the first decades of the new century. Some had even advanced to "white collar" status. Lingering prejudices and the stagnant economy of the Depression era limited their progress, however, and prevented their full integration into American society.

The Irish were among the prime beneficiaries of the more open and fluid American society generated by the Second World War. Already having a foot up on the ladder of social mobility, they took advantage of the G.I. Bill of Rights and other postwar benefits to such effect that record numbers of young men of immigrant stock obtained the college degrees and suburban homes that had remained beyond the grasp, or even the dreams, of their fathers. Advanced education, further training, automobiles, readily available mortgages, a postwar spirit of expectancy and optimism—all these led to new jobs and new neighborhoods, and the breakup of tight-knit ethnic enclaves.

By 1960, the suburbanization of the Irish was well underway. People who had learned to identify themselves by mentioning the urban parish in which they were born, and where they went to school, married, and raised their children, were now driving out to the hinterlands to visit their children and grand-children, or, in many cases, moving there themselves. City churches bearing the names of Irish saints were experiencing decline in their congregations, or were surviving with a new population of later immigrants. South Boston and a few other old neighborhoods defied the trend, but throughout the country, the "Irishtowns" were disappearing, the Irish along with them.

James T. Farrell.

Alfred E. Smith, governor of New York and presidential nominee, shown in conversation with baseball hero Babe Ruth in 1923.

FROM SMITH TO KENNEDY

Alfred E. Smith was the wrong man, at the wrong time. The presidency of the United States was, of course, the ultimate political prize, and the Irish, as "America's political class," had always aspired to that eminence. They had enjoyed the courtship of presidential candidates from Andrew Jackson onward who had alluded to their Irish ancestry, but these worthies (including Theodore Roosevelt and Woodrow Wilson) had targeted their ethnic appeals very precisely to Irish audiences and taken care not to publicize their "Irishness" to the general public. Moreover, the half dozen or so presidents with roots in Ireland had all belonged to the "Scotch-Irish" Protestant population that most Americans did not consider really Irish at all. Aside from the distinguished lawyer, Charles O'Conor, who won nearly thirty thousand votes as the nominee of a Democratic splinter party in 1872, no Irish Catholic had ever ventured into the ultimate political arena.

By the 1920s the time seemed ripe. Refused the nomination in 1924, "Al" Smith gained it in 1928, and ran against Herbert Hoover, the "Great Engineer" of prosperity, as Secretary of Commerce under two Republican presidents.

On paper, Smith seemed well-qualified. An experienced legislator and administrator, he had been an effective governor of the nation's most populous state. But he was also a product of the Tammany machine, a protégé of "Boss" Murphy, and—worst of all, from a national perspective—the epitome of urban, Catholic, anti-Prohibition Irish assertiveness. Born on

New York's Lower East Side (and actually only part Irish), Smith had the accent, manners, style, and attitude that could still antagonize voters all the way from the rural redneck to the haunts of the gentry.

Although there were many factors responsible for Smith's defeat, including the soon-to-be-exploded illusions of "Coolidge prosperity," Smith's own persona, the stereotype it invoked, and the lingering fear of "Popery" were enough to doom him. The country was still not ready for an Irish Catholic president—at least not one who looked and sounded like Al Smith—and where was any alternative to be found among the ranks of Irish Catholic politicians?

The Irish political presence during the New Deal period ranged from flamboyant old-time "machine" figures, like James Michael Curley of

FIRST · CAR

Henry Ford in his first automobile. **Henry Ford was the father of America's greatest industry and founder of what is still one of its major companies. Ford's father left County Cork during the Famine era, and the Ford automobile company opened a branch company in that part of Ireland seventy years later.**

Boston, to behind-the-scenes advisers of the Roosevelt administration, like Thomas Corcoran. Among the governors, congressmen, and wire-pullers, however, there appeared no personality of presidential caliber.

James A. Farley of New York, to be sure, clearly aspired to the White House. As national chairman of the Democratic Party, and Roosevelt's Postmaster-General, "Big Jim" demonstrated that his political and managerial skills were considerable. But, ultimately, he was shrewd enough to realize that his party was not ready to nominate, or his country to elect, a man of his background to the highest office in the land.

Another Irish American who dallied with presidential dreams during this period was Joseph P. Kennedy. An immigrant's grandson, a Harvard graduate, a son-in-law of Boston's mayor "Honey Fitz" Fitzgerald, a multimillionaire, a supporter of FDR who had been rewarded with the London embassy (though he believed he deserved a Cabinet post), and a relentless manipulator in both business and politics, "Joe" Kennedy eventually adopted a realistic view of his own limited prospects in Washington. Instead, he conceived the seemingly just-as-fantastic idea of making his son the first Irish Catholic president of the United States.

John Fitzgerald Kennedy emerged from World War II as an authentic naval hero, and his father's choice (following the death of an older brother) for the presidency. Within fifteen years, after terms in the House of Representatives and the Senate, "JFK" had attained that goal.

The story of John F. Kennedy's triumph and tragedy is well-known: family support, personal charisma, political skill, popular adulation, international glamour, and a career cut short by assassination, leaving historians puzzling over how to assess its substance. In the context of the Irish immigrant experience, Kennedy's 1960 electoral victory can be understood in either of two ways.

Some analysts hail the winning of the White House as the culmination of the centuries'-long quest of the American Irish for acceptance. In this ver-

James Farley with James, Jr.

sion, the Irish have been so thoroughly assimilated that an Irish Catholic can at last be chosen on his own merits. On the other hand, it has been pointed out, JFK was utterly atypical of his ethnic group. A rich, prep school– and Ivy League–educated, charming, and witty sophisticate, he had all the ease and eloquence to which many Irish could lay claim, seemingly without the rough edges. He was so unlike Al Smith that he seemed to be from another planet.

The crucial issue, of course, was the Catholicism to which so many of the American Irish still clung, and which set them apart, in a multitude of both obvious and subtle ways from their fellow citizens. For Smith, whatever the depth of his personal convictions, religion had been a burden that weighed him down beyond remedy. For Kennedy, religion was worn lightly, and the profound doubts that many non-Catholics still held about the political trustworthiness of Roman Catholics were suspended after such reassuring exchanges as Kennedy's famous meeting with a group of Protestant clergymen in which he dismissed the inherent conflicts

President Kennedy in a light-hearted moment as his children dressed in Halloween costumes visit him in the oval office.

between religious and secular responsibilities with a few well-chosen generalizations. Smith had been accused of plotting to build a tunnel to the Vatican; Kennedy, one wag observed, could probably have tacked the project onto an appropriation bill without any serious protests being raised.

Kennedy—who, it must be remembered, did not win by a landslide—was able to attain the presidency because he was so unlike a typical Irishman, and his Catholicism seemed so bland, so unthreatening. If we look at JFK from the perspective of the average American, we do not see the "acceptable" Irish American, but, rather, a generic celebrity.

Viewed in this light, the achievement of the presidency by John F. Kennedy revealed a simple formula for the Irish to succeed in America: "Vanish!"

The Joseph P. Kennedy family, c. 1960. From the beginning the Irish have been unusually prominent and successful in American politics.

A CLOSER LOOK:
ISLAND
Edited with permission of Beaver Island
Historical Society and Helen Collar

It was in the Irish quarters of eastern cities that those who were the first to come to Beaver Island heard about the Michigan isle that was to be their future home. Later, many came directly to the island, having been sent for by relatives.

Beaver Island has been a place for the gathering of the clans from the 1860s. Ties of blood and friendship were strong, ties that had been forged in the close knit island communities of their Irish homeland. The new island reminded them of the old; in family after family the words have come down, "it was like Ireland." But, unlike Ireland, here in America there was not only good fishing, but also land so cheap even a poor man could buy, a much prized

boon that had been denied them in their native land. Word first went to friends and relatives already in the United States and Canada, but it was not long before letters were sent to Ireland. Later some Beaver Islanders made trips back to Aranmore and Rutland, and there extolled the wonders of their American island. The virtues of Beaver lost nothing in the telling, and the stories of the visitors took deep root in the islands off the coast of Donegal. The words "Beaver Island" have a magical effect in Aranmore, opening doors and producing smiles and a hearty welcome to visitors from afar. Old men tell tales of an island they have never seen, but that they firmly believed to be a veritable Garden of Eden.

The Monahan Men's Dancing School, 1910–20.
Perfecting social skills became a necessary step in the assimilation process.

A CLOSER LOOK:
CHARACTERS

For a region not usually thought of as a haven for Irish immigrants, the South has produced a fair share of writers of Irish descent, from Kate (Flaherty) Chopin to Flannery O'Connor. Even more notable is the fact that two of the most famous characters in American fiction are Southerners of Irish origin: Huckleberry Finn and Scarlett O'Hara.

Mark Twain presumably brought neither ethnic insight nor much personal acquaintance to his image of Huck, but he is the son of a drunkard named Pat Finn, and for most nineteenth-century Americans, what could be more Irish than that? A picaresque wanderer, venturesome and superstitious, shrewd and naive, full of instinctive prejudices toward his black companion, Jim, but also ready to show him human respect, Huck is, whether or not by design, full of Irish traits.

Katherine Scarlett O'Hara, the daughter of an immigrant from Wexford, owes her ancestry to Margaret Mitchell's own Irish roots. Gerald O'Hara frequently reminds "Katy Scarlett" of *her* roots, pointing out that because she is Irish, the land is her life, and indeed, it is to Tara that she returns after all her adventures, to find strength for "another day." In the interim, she has lied, cheated, killed, made a fortune, and lost three husbands—a resourceful survivor, in the best Irish tradition.

Be it Scarlett O'Hara fleeing from devastated Atlanta, or Huckleberry Finn rafting down the Mississippi, the Old South, in its own special way, offers a home away from home to the ever-restless Gaels.

One of the greatest
song- and dance-men
ever, Gene Kelly revels
in the singin', the
dancin', and the rain in
this favorite scene from
the movie *Singin' in the
Rain*.

(Left) George M.
Cohan, here portrayed
by James Cagney,
in a 1942 Warner Bros.
production of *Yankee
Doodle Dandy,* directed
by Walter Huston.

(Below) Poster for the
colorful production of
Yankee Doodle Dandy.

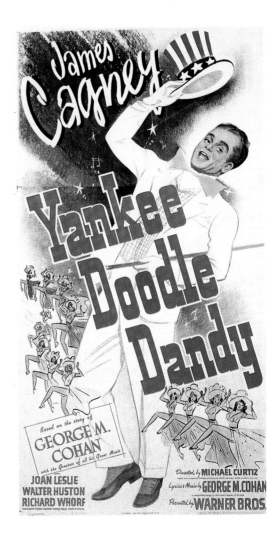

The Last Hurrah, a John Ford production with Spencer Tracy and Pat O'Brien, tells the story of Boston's Mayor Curley.

(Above) Spencer Tracy inspects the police commissioners of Omaha's famous Boys Town while the MGM company was on location there for scenes in *Boys Town* starring Tracy and Mickey Rooney.

(Right) Spencer Tracy and Mickey Rooney in *Boys Town*.

A CLOSER LOOK:
DIRECTOR

Born in Maine to Irish immigrant parents, Sean Aloysius O'Fearna wisely adopted the more manageable name of *John Ford* when he began his filmmaking career, but he never forgot his Irish roots.

From his directorial debut with *The Tornado* (1917) , when he was barely twenty-three, through *The Iron Horse* (1924), the classic *Stagecoach* (1939), and on to the cavalry and Indian epics of the 1940s and 1950s, he displayed his passion for American history, particularly in its western dimension. Many of these films weave in the Irish participation in the making of America, and among the actors one sees again and again are the members of what came to be known as Ford's "Irish-American stock company."

For two of his best-known works, the director went directly to settings in Ireland. *The Informer* (1935), set in the bleak environment of Dublin during the "Troubles," follows its simple-minded protagonist as he tries to obtain money for a passage to America by betraying a rebel leader to the British authorities, and flees the torment of remorse as well as the vengeance of the IRA. While few would question the artistry of this Academy Award–winning film, *The Quiet Man* (1953) is less universally esteemed. Its hero is a returned "Yank," who grew up in America, had a career in boxing, and now seeks a quiet life. He becomes embroiled in various romantic and comic situations, and the climax is a long, drawn out fistfight that extends over much of the town and surrounding countryside. Some regard *The Quiet Man* as overly sentimental, filled with stereotypical characters and situations. It remains, however, the vehicle by which a whole generation of Americans, of all ethnic backgrounds, arrived at an amiable awareness of Ireland and the Irish.

Ford was the recipient of three Academy Awards, and received the American Film Institute's first Life Achievement Award in 1973, the year of his death.

(Background) **John Ford and Clark Gable in** *Mogambo,* **1953.**

(Above) **Victor McLaglen in** *The Informer,* **directed by John Ford, 1935.**

(Right) **John Ford directing** *Young Cassidy,* **July 1964.**

(Far right) **Maureen O'Hara and John Wayne in the Oscar-winning 1952 film** *The Quiet Man,* **directed by John Ford.**

(Above) Gregory Peck and John Huston read *Moby Dick* comic books to the children at St. Mary's Home in New Bedford, Massachusetts prior to the premiere of the Huston-directed film *Moby Dick*.

(Left) Walter Huston listens attentively as his son, John, discusses a scene from *We Were Strangers* with Jennifer Jones.

John Huston leads the parade of animals as Noah in his epic treatment of *The Bible*. Special trenches along the procession route enable handlers to keep the beasts in line while remaining unseen to the camera's eye.

John Wayne's commanding presence in *The Sons of Katie Elder.*

Paul Newman as Butch Cassidy with Robert Redford in *Butch Cassidy and the Sundance Kid.*

THE AMERICAN IRISH RENAISSANCE (1960–   )

That endangered species, the Irish in the United States, was saved from vanishing into a homogeneous "American" core population by three developments.

The first was the reemergence of the age-old "Irish Question" in a particularly violent and persistent form. The second was a general upsurge in ethnic consciousness among Americans who rebelled against the looming loss of their distinctive identities. The third was the arrival of a new generation of immigrants—not always readily integrated with those of an earlier era, but unquestionably a vital stimulant to the consciousness of those who had lost touch with the "old country."

"ULSTER WILL FIGHT"

For more than a hundred years, the Protestants of Ireland's North have repeated the slogans voiced against Parnell's Home Rule plan of the 1880s: "Home Rule means Rome Rule," "No Surrender," "Ulster will Fight," and "Ulster will be Right."

When Ireland was partitioned in the 1920s, six of Ulster's traditional nine counties became Northern Ireland, an entity created to ease the anxieties of Irish Protestants by perpetuating their link to Britain in an area where

(Previous spread) **A respect for tradition and devotion to family brought the Murphy clan together at the family home in Norfolk, Connecticut, 1988.**

(Opposite) **Liam Neeson in** *Michael Collins.* **The critical and popular success of the film is due in part to the enthusiasm for Irish subjects and themes.**

they were a majority. For the Unionists this movement preserved the only assurance of safety against the "Popish hordes" that dominated the rest of the island. Although Nationalists ranted against partition, and the Irish Republican Army launched futile guerrilla campaigns in 1940 and the late 1950s, the Northern Ireland province of the United Kingdom survived its first four decades unscathed and seemingly impervious to external criticism or internal discontent.

By the early 1960s, most Americans of Irish origin were indifferent to the existence of Northern Ireland. Those of Protestant heritage (chiefly of Ulster Scots descent) had, for the most part, slid into the American population, leaving little trace of their Irishness behind.

Nor did Catholics pay a great deal of attention to the status of their co-religionists in the North. To the extent that they concerned themselves with Ireland at all, they preferred to concentrate on the positive news from the Republic of Ireland, where a rise in prosperity had reversed the post-war pattern of decline. Economic growth, built on foreign investment and improved management of tourism, had produced new employment

Mrs. McSwiney, sister of the late Lord Mayor of Dublin, being taken to the police station after protesting in front of the British Embassy, Washington, D.C., November 1922.

opportunities and a renewed sense of optimism in the twenty-six counties. Moreover, Ireland was winning respect as an active member of the United Nations, with peace-keeping troops in the Congo and diplomats serving as international policy makers. Ireland and Britain had moved closer since the bitterness caused by De Valera's wartime neutrality stance, and the two governments were planning joint initiatives in the realm of European economic cooperation. Even the Belfast regime had come to the point of making friendly overtures toward Dublin. The two prime ministers had exchanged visits to each other's capitals, and cross-border cooperation was increasing. Indeed, many academic and cultural bodies had long since created pan-Irish committees and conferences that transcended the political boundary. When the fiftieth anniversary of the Easter Rising was solemnly marked in 1966, there was a mood of optimism as well as of nostalgic nationalism evident in speeches and editorials. To all but the most passionate foes of partition, things seemed to be getting better every day, in every way. Irish Americans found it easy to be lulled into a reassured indifference to conditions in Northern Ireland.

Few Americans understood the realities of life in Northern Ireland. The Catholic minority (about one-third of the population) were subject to political gerrymandering that denied them a full share in the democratic process. Worse, they were subject to socioeconomic discrimination that denied them equal access to the benefits of the British Welfare State.

Irish-American protesters march in front of the Immigration building in Boston to protest deportation of Irish nationalists who were formerly prisoners in Britain.

193

Public housing and employment were allocated so as to favor Protestant applicants.

The basis for anti-Catholic discrimination was not simply the belief that they were all ardent nationalists, potential traitors to the United Kingdom longing for a thirty-two-county Irish Republic—an assumption that was by no means universally valid. Ulstermen nursed a deep-seated animosity against "Popery," derived from more than three centuries of sectarian strife. Religious differences which in other countries no longer aroused interest, much less passion, were kept alive in Ulster by preachers and teachers. Annual rituals commemorated seventeenth-century Protestant victories over Catholics, and parades through Catholic districts by members of the Loyal Orange Order reminded the minority of past humiliation and present subjugation. Banners, political harangues, and repeated chants that amounted to war cries all spoke of a historical hatred that was carefully maintained.

The demonization of Northern Ireland's Catholic minority went beyond labeling them "Republican" and "Popish," however. It took on the character of racism, despite the virtual identity in appearance and accent between Northerners of the two confessional groups. According to the prevailing stereotype, the Catholic was lazy, unreliable, ignorant, superstitious, and dirty. He bred many children and lived in squalor. Such images were used to justify segregated neighborhoods and exclusion from all but the most menial jobs.

As virtually all residents of Northern Ireland attended Church-run schools, there was little opportunity for children to encounter those of different religious backgrounds, and generations had grown up accepting the folklore transmitted by their families. Indeed, employers who wished to discriminate in hiring could apply sectarian bias merely by noting what school a job-hunter had attended, without having to specifically ask about his or her religion.

Only at the university was there even a chance for young Northern Irelanders to move across sectarian barriers. Many working-class boys and girls, taking advantage of British government subsidies, had ventured into the halls of higher education by the 1960s. There they found not only the opportunity to interact on a friendly basis with people of the other side of the sectarian divide, but they were able to encounter a wider range of ideas and a broader awareness of the world outside Ulster than had come their way in childhood. It was from the ranks of these university students that many of the activists who launched the Northern Ireland civil rights movement emerged.

Father and daughter in a demonstration against the deportation of former Irish political prisoners now living in the U.S.

It was African-Americans rather than Irish Americans who inspired the renewal of Ireland's struggle with Britain. The example of black civil rights marchers and demonstrators in the segregationist strongholds of the United States struck home with the despised and disenfranchised of Northern Ireland, who saw clear parallels between the discrimination practiced against the minority in places like Alabama and Georgia and that directed against the minority in Ulster. As in the American South, activists in the Irish North often came from the politically sensitized and reform-oriented ranks of students and recent university graduates. There were frequent references to themselves as "the blacks of Ireland" and a readiness to borrow slogans, or songs like "We Shall Overcome," and apply them to the Ulster situation.

The founding of the Northern Ireland Civil Rights Association in 1967 was followed by a series of demonstrations demanding equality for Catholics in access to employment, housing, and equity in franchise. In October 1968 demonstrators clashed with the Royal Ulster Constabulary, the almost entirely Protestant police force of Northern Ireland, and the first blows were struck in the new "Troubles." In January 1969 a civil rights march from Belfast to Londonderry was attacked by Protestant stone-throwers; the police made no attempt to protect the marchers. Riots, attacks on Catholic neighborhoods, and the "burning out" of Catholic families in Belfast prompted the British government to send troops into the province in August. Although they were at first welcomed as protectors by the Catholics, the heavy-handed tactics of these military units soon made them seem almost as biased and oppressive as the police. By early 1970, after nearly a decade of passivity, the Irish Republican Army was counterattacking the "British army of occupation." A new war had broken out in Ireland.

The renewal of Ireland's "Troubles" in 1968 revived the phenomenon of "Irish America." Only a handful of old-timers and a few recent immigrants had kept the Fenian flame alive, since the founding of the Free State seemed to have resolved the Irish Question. Since the Second World War, the "Irish vote" had virtually ceased to sway Washington policymakers, who realized that the number of Americans who claimed Irish descent on census forms bore little relation to the number who took only conscious interest in the matter of partition.

Suddenly, Ireland was "news." The American media, along with their coverage of violence in Southeast Asia, Latin America, and the Middle East, began regular reporting on the Northern Ireland conflict.

The struggle in Ireland lent itself particularly well to the demands of television, which, from the 1970s onward, became America's principal source of news and information: gun battles, rock-throwing children, bombed buildings, enraged youths, mournful mothers, prayerful clergymen, and shoulder-shrugging academics all passed across the screen week-in and

This boy in Derry is one of the latest generation of rebels in Northern Ireland, July 1996.

week-out, raising America's awareness that something dreadful was happening in a land they had come to dismiss as a quiet backwater.

If the general public in the United States could no longer ignore the woes of Ulster, how much less could the Irish-descended population? When their ancestral homeland was being torn by strife, when the partition of Ireland had again become a matter of urgent dispute, how could Irish Americans remain complacent in their "vanished" status? The American Irish reacted to the new "Troubles" in a wide variety of ways. Some young zealots (and a few not so young) actually made their way to Ireland and joined the "armed struggle." Such amateur enthusiasts were more trouble than they were worth to the IRA: a secret army can find little use for such ill-prepared and attention-grabbing recruits. More helpful were those who supplied financial backing, smuggled weapons, or provided transatlantic refuges for IRA men on the run from the British government. A broad support network for the "Republican cause" was built up, stretching from coast to coast, and including third- and fourth-generation "Yanks" as well as immigrants and the children of immigrants. Some organizations, such as the Irish Northern Aid Committee (NORAID) collected donations openly, insisting that these funds were used exclusively for charitable pur-

**Daniel Day Lewis
(right) portraying an
Irish political prisoner
in *In the Name of the
Father*. The appeal of
this and similar films
on the revived Irish
Question to American
audiences is part
of the phenomenon
of renewed Irish con-
sciousness in the
United States.**

poses, such as relieving the distress of persecuted "Republican" families in
Ulster. Whether or not one preferred to hear these disclaimers before
making a contribution, there were plenty of channels to keep money
flowing to Ireland. London might complain to Washington, and the FBI
might pursue investigations, or even make arrests, but the "cause" never
lacked loyal backers.

Irish orators loved to speak of the eight-hundred-year fight against
England's tyranny, but few listeners had ever thought seriously about the
agony of a war that dragged on for decades. The death and destruction, the
weariness and sheer futility of the war of liberation that began in 1969,
stretched on through the 1970s, the 1980s, and on into the 1990s with
seemingly no end in sight. Periodically, some dramatic episode would raise
the level of shock and rage: the "Bloody Sunday" shooting of seventeen
Catholic protesters by British troops; the brutal circumstances under
which ten IRA prisoners starved themselves to death while demanding
political rather than criminal status. The Northern Ireland government was
replaced by direct British rule, Protestant paramilitary groups like the
"Ulster Defense Force" took reprisals against real or supposed nationalists,
and the IRA carried its campaign of shooting and bombing into Britain,
as well as continental Europe. The death toll exceeded three thousand—

mostly civilians, caught in the crossfire. All efforts at a negotiated settlement based upon some formula for sharing power ended in failure. Where could a resolution of this seemingly endless torment be found?

For a newly self-aware Irish-American population, the answer was clear: in the United States—not in fund-raising, moral support, or even prayers for peace, but, rather, in the persuasive power of the American presidency. Ironically, all the presidents of this period, except one (George Bush) had Irish roots. Richard Nixon and Ronald Reagan made much of visiting ancestral graves on their trips to Ireland. Yet repeated cries from Irish-American governors, senators, and congressmen—to say nothing of organizations—failed to produce a consistent and aggressively pursued policy toward the Ulster conflict. Aside from moral exhortations and the occasional encouragement of American investment to revive the depressed economy of Northern Ireland, none of the successive administrations, Democratic or Republican, would risk the "special relationship" between the United States and Britain by intruding upon the internal affairs of the United Kingdom. Sympathy for the sufferings of those caught up in the conflict was dismissed as naive acquiescence in IRA propaganda, while those who sought to pressure Washington into demanding constructive action were denounced as supporters of terrorism.

Early in his first term, President Clinton meets with Sinn Fein president Gerry Adams to emphasize U.S. interest in a Northern Ireland peace process.

William D. Griffin, co-founder and first president of the U.S. Irish History Roundtable, meets with Mary Robinson, president of the Republic of Ireland, during ceremonies commemorating the tenth anniversary of the Roundtable's establishment, October 1994.

Even the end of the Cold War did not alter the administration's resolve to avoid offending Britain by taking a strong line on the Irish Question. The almost symbiotic relationship between Prime Minister Margaret Thatcher and President Ronald Reagan guaranteed that her hard line in Ulster would not be disputed, and Britain's staunch support of the United States in the Gulf War of 1990–1991 assured a continuing commitment from the Bush White House.

The presidential campaign of 1992 at long last offered the possibility of a shift in policy. The Democratic Party's nominee, Bill Clinton, making much of his Irish ancestry (his mother was a Cassidy), promised Irish-American activists that he would, if elected, pursue an active policy aimed at a peaceful resolution of the conflict in Northern Ireland. Nationalist sympathizers hailed his promises as the clearest, most straightforward statement from any major politician in decades. Cynics dismissed Clinton's promises as a mere rhetorical bid to reanimate the old "Irish vote," which had dissipated, or realigned itself under other banners in recent years. When Clinton won the 1992 election, the doubters at first seemed to be justified in their skepticism, for no overt policy initiatives appeared to be forthcoming, even though the British government had blatantly favored the reelection of Clinton's opponent.

By the end of 1993, however, the Irish-American hopes were revived, when the president began promoting the idea of an all-party conference in Northern Ireland to resolve the conflict. Like the "Peace Process" in the

Middle East, aimed at settling the Arab-Israeli struggle, the Clinton administration's initiative recognized the special role and obligation of the United States, as the world's only remaining superpower, to foster the peaceful resolution of regional conflicts. But both peace processes acknowledged the particular concern of significant communities within the United States in ending bloodshed in their "homelands." During the protracted Northern Ireland troubles, newly invigorated Irish-American organizations had frequently complained that the problems of Israel were given more consistent and intensive attention than those of Ireland—an equation more emotional than realistic. In any case, once launched, the American policy was steadily pursued, through a series of advances and setbacks, from 1994 through 1996. The IRA proclaimed a cease-fire, abandoned it, and then renewed it. Its political wing, Sinn Fein, was, for the first time, invited to peace talks, then uninvited, then reinvited. Nationalist and Unionist factions postured and maneuvered, new regimes won power in London and Dublin. And despite all, the Americans patiently persisted in encouraging negotiations, with former Senator George Mitchell of Maine, himself of Irish extraction, serving as the president's special representative on Northern Ireland.

Finally, in September 1997, all-party talks were convened in Belfast, and a new phase of the peace process began. Whatever the ultimate outcome, it was America's long-delayed intervention that broke the deadlock, and it was the persistent demands of the American Irish that won this vital response from the White House. At the end of the day, the American Irish, in fighting for peace and justice in Northern Ireland, had reasserted themselves as a distinct people within the American mosaic.

AMERICAN IRISH CULTURE RECLAIMED

Interwoven with the moral outrage and political passion that the Northern Ireland conflict reawakened in so many Irish Americans was a sense of belonging to a distinctive cultural tradition that set them apart from other citizens of the United States.

Such thoughts might have been deemed unpatriotic, or at least a poor choice for those intent upon social and economic advancement, only a few years earlier. The stimulus provided by the Ulster crisis, however, coincided with what can only be described as a craze for ethnicity, and the Irish found that being a "hyphenated American" was no longer unacceptable.

It may be that the Irish, like other ethnic groups, had simply grown weary of the homogenizing tendencies of American life. What is clear is that the television series "Roots," based on Alex Haley's account of his search for his family's origins, had an impact far beyond the African-American population that was the focus of his narrative. The enthusiasm for searching out one's family history spread across all America's ethnic and racial groups. Moreover, "Roots research," as it was popularly called, went far beyond the limited (and often self-congratulatory) investigations of genealogical hob-

Bono, lead singer of the Irish rock band U2, performs in concert with bandmate Adam Clayton, 1997.

byists. It interwove with the rise of the new social history approaches of academia, which favored an emphasis on women, children, everyday life, and various marginal, neglected groups. Family history became part of a broader concern with origins and development of the various groups that made up American society. What would have been dismissed in the 1950s as retrograde or trivial became in the 1970s legitimate, and even fashionable. Wide-ranging amateurs and narrowly focused scholars, who had ignored or even despised one another, now displayed respect, or even shared information.

By the early 1990s, more than two hundred colleges and universities, in all parts of the United States, were offering courses in various aspects of Irish culture, including history, literature, folklore, and music. Encouraged by student demands, some universities introduced entire degree programs in Irish studies. Professors who had been obliged to earn their way as teachers of British history or "English literature" were suddenly in demand as specialists in Irish civilization. The American Committee for Irish Studies, which had started life modestly in the 1960s as a discussion group for a handful of academics, grew by the 1990s into an interdisciplinary "conference" of more than a thousand members, holding an annual national meeting, with a week-long series of lectures and seminars, as well as half a dozen regional chapters, each with its own program.

Many mixed groups of "professional" and amateur students of Irish culture sprang up throughout the country, typified by the New York Irish History Roundtable, founded in 1984. Its particular interest is the three-hundred-year experience of Irish immigrants and their descendants in the New York City area. In addition to regular meetings, its several hundred members promote research and documentation, through newsletters, an annual journal, and a series of major publications in the field of New York Irish history.

The reclamation of Irish culture in America went far beyond the tracing of ancestors and the documentation of ethnic history. Classes in the Gaelic language proliferated, and a market for books, both old and new, in that nearly extinct language developed. Gaelic tapes and videos were also increasingly in demand. Like Gaelic language classes, which were often privately organized outside a school setting, many Irish Americans chose to acquaint themselves with contemporary poetry, prose, and drama firsthand, either by visiting Ireland, or by attending the performances and readings given by the growing number of Irish actors and writers who toured the United States.

Traditional Irish music and dance also experienced a striking revival. Both visiting performers and American-generated groups drew even larger audiences. Unlike the cliché-ridden "Irish" musical shows of the 1940s and 1950s, the musical experiences of the renewed consciousness encompassed both the very old, such as archaic Celtic instruments, taken up again after centuries of neglect, and the new, among them the latest Irish (or American Irish) rock groups, or the new-Celtic productions of troupers like *Riverdance*.

The Irish renaissance of the 1970s and 1980s brought new life to the fading radio programs that had hitherto appealed chiefly to aging immigrants. New (and livelier) content, combined with regular coverage of events in Ireland, drew an audience from the rising generation. Established radio shows were supplemented by new programs, with dynamic and inventive hosts, often in previously untouched areas, such as the Far West. Television, more cautious in exploring the new "Irish market," nonetheless experimented with a number of offerings outside of the familiar St. Patrick's Day "specials," and even offered programs produced in Ireland. Filmmakers, who had virtually abandoned Irish themes by the 1950s, took them up again as the doings of the IRA generated scripts on everything from terrorism to dysfunctional families. The historical background to Ireland's contemporary woes was explored in such films as *Michael Collins,* and even the seamier side of Irish-American society, virtually unseen since the heyday of Jimmy Cagney, found its way back to the screen, reminding moviegoers that the American Irish had spawned their fair share of gangsters and sociopaths.

Irish-American women are increasingly joining their male counterparts in the legal and judicial professions. Here, Sandra Day O'Connor stands next to Supreme Court Chief Justice Warren Burger at her first day on the job as a Supreme Court Justice, Sept. 25, 1981.

Irish America's once-thriving ethnic newspapers had withered to a puny remnant by the 1950s. Here again the new Irish consciousness of the 1970s reversed a negative trend. By the 1990s there were "Irish" newspapers published on both coasts, with New York City sustaining two weeklies that exhibited high standards of journalistic professionalism and community service. Numerous magazines also made their appearance during this period, some merely ephemeral, but others, notably *Irish America*, maintaining a consistently high level of content and vitality. In addition, newspapers and magazines from Ireland gained a wider readership in the United States, and became increasingly available in shops catering to "Irish-interest" readers.

American book publishers, too, looked with increasing favor at manuscripts on Irish themes, in fields ranging from history to humor, and even reprinted old titles, a sure sign that publishers recognized the expansion of an "Irish-oriented" reading public.

Riding the wave of the revival, the Irish-American Cultural Institute grew from a midwestern college-based publisher of newsletters in the 1970s into a multiactivity enterprise that distributed books, organized tours, arranged lectures by visiting Irish luminaries, and facilitated study in Ireland by American students. In more recent years, the Institute has awarded grants to promote research in Irish studies, and along with other organizations, such as the Ireland Fund, has channeled American benefactions into cultural and development projects in Ireland.

Paul O'Neill continues the tradition of Irish-American participation in baseball.

The new emphasis on Irish culture did not depend on initiatives from the community. Museums and galleries that paid little or no attention to things Irish in the past discovered a new dimension for their exhibitions. New York's Metropolitan Museum of Art, for example, staged *Treasures of Early Irish Art,* in which it hosted the Book of Kells and dozens of other medieval masterpieces on loan from Dublin collections. Irish and Irish-American painters and sculptors were featured in highly praised shows during the 1980s, while *The Gaelic Gotham* presentation at the Museum of the City of New York drew widespread attention to the history of the Irish in the metropolis, while sparking bitter controversy during 1995 and 1996.

The more overtly commercial dimensions of the Irish cultural resurgence included a nationwide proliferation of pubs and restaurants featuring "typical" Irish ambiance and fare, and catering to Irish Americans or "those who wished they were Irish." Irish clothing designers and artisans found new outlets in America, thanks to nationwide promotions, such as that staged by Bloomingdale's in 1981. Tourist promotion, trade shows, and energetic public relations campaigns, reflecting a growing sophistication in these areas by representatives of the Irish government, in cooperation with American business and media interests, have steadily enhanced the image of Ireland as a good—and safe—place to visit or conduct business. This positive image has, in turn, stirred the pride and encouraged the involvement of Irish Americans who, a generation earlier, might have dismissed the condition of Ireland as irrelevant to their own lives.

Sneers about plastic shamrocks and green beer on St. Patrick's Day may continue, but they are less frequent, and less on target, than they were a few decades ago. The level of Irish-American cultural awareness and the

intelligent, thoughtful celebration of a heritage once in danger of being lost, show every evidence of increase.

General Colin Powell, former Chairman of the Joint Chiefs of Staff.

"JUST OFF THE PLANE"

The Irish in America had been reinforced and renewed for more than a century by an annual influx of immigrants when that flow diminished drastically in the 1920s. Newcomers, "just off the boat," were always good for a laugh, with their naive credulity and their confused responses to the wonders of "the States" not only amusing, but gratifying to the egos of those who had been here long enough to learn the ropes. But once they stopped coming, at least in any significant numbers, the Irishness of the Irish Americans was inevitably diminished, and yet another factor was added to the assimilation process. In this context the coming of a new generation of immigrants during the last quarter of the twentieth century played a vital role, along with political and cultural factors, in stimulating the Irish renaissance in America.

The irregular, but generally decreasing pattern of Irish immigration from the mid-1920s onward was drastically affected by quota adjustments in 1965, which cut the average annual intake to under two thousand. This limitation hit hard during the 1970s, as the economic upturn of Ireland's previous decade was reversed, and unemployment led many to look, as so often in the past, across the Atlantic. The late 1970s and early 1980s became the "days of the undocumented." With normal immigration virtually impossible due to long waiting lists of applicants, the Irish adopted the strategies of other nationalities, ranging from clandestine border crossings to the most common device: the presentation of a visitor's visa. Young Irish men and women, often well-educated and possessing advanced job skills, would enter the United States on a short-term basis, pretending to be tourists or Irish cousins paying a two-week call on their American kinfolk. Once in the country, they would disappear into the underground of "illegals."

Many of these visa-overstayers went virtually unsought by the Immigration and Naturalization Service, which seemed preoccupied with tracing down Latin American and other "Third World" immigrants, while leaving the Irish (and most other Europeans) undisturbed.

By some estimates, nearly one hundred thousand illegal immigrants from Ireland entered the United States between the early 1970s and the mid-1980s, when a new law providing additional residential visas eased the problem. As long as they remained undocumented, they were obliged to live in a shadowy environment of temporary jobs as laborers, baby-sitters, and bar or restaurant workers, using forged papers and dodging contacts with even the most harmless of government agencies. They sought to blend into the host society by remaining in the surviving "old neighborhoods," such as South Boston or New York's Woodside, though it would not require any great ingenuity on the part of INS agents to spot a young person with a marked Irish accent as a likely candidate for deportation.

By the early 1990s, a more generous distribution of residential visas had begun to introduce a new breed of "new" Irish immigrants: able to turn

Tip O'Neill, as the Speaker of the House.

their talents to a wide variety of occupations, and free to roam about the country, they might turn up anywhere from California to Florida, as anything from cameramen to chefs. Moreover, the Ireland that they had left, often with the intention of merely "exploring" America for a few years and refining their skills, was now a full-fledged and newly prospering member of a European union that was moving toward full economic integration. The Irish men and women of the 1990s, "just off the plane" from the "old country," enjoyed more options than, and might well exhibit different attitudes from, those who had arrived a decade or so earlier, but like them they contributed to the revitalization of the Irish presence in America. These new arrivals brought a new immediacy to the role of being Irish in America, maintained an ongoing demand for the cultural and informational fruits of the post-1960's renaissance, and contributed to the generational tensions than can damage—but also stimulate—an ethnic community.

A CLOSER LOOK:
MAGAZINE

They said it couldn't be done. Prophets of doom asserted that a magazine aimed at the Irish-American community had no chance of success. Nevertheless, publisher Niall O'Dowd and editor Patricia Harty went ahead with the founding of *Irish America* in 1985. As they passed their twelfth anniversary they had the readership and the financial prosperity to prove the critics wrong.

The magazine seeks to promote a better awareness of contemporary Ireland among the Irish in America, to tell the Irish of the accomplishments and experiences of their brethren in the U.S., and to give an honest picture of the ongoing problems in Northern Ireland. It features a mixture of articles, illustrations, and features that are balanced with an accessible tone. Among long-term goals, Patricia Harty says, are an increased amount of poetry and fiction and the introduction of Irish language material.

The editor is optimistic, but realistic. A native of Tipperary, Harty realizes that a certain amount of bad poetry is in circulation, and that a certain amount of Irish language instruction may be needed along with the features in that language. Nonetheless, *Irish America* has achieved a distinctive place in the renaissance of the Irish-American community and through a shrewd combination of innovation and awareness of past achievements and pitfalls has created bright prospects for the future.

(Background, this page) Anchorman Tom Brokaw and publisher Niall O'Dowd at *Irish America*'s Top 100 Awards, 1995.

(Above) Irish writers Tim Pat Coogan, Edna O'Brien and Frank McCourt, 1997.

(Right) Donald Keough, president emeritus of Coca-Cola, Natasha Richardson, her husband, Irish actor Liam Neeson, and Patricia Harty, editor-in-chief.

(Opposite) Magazine co-founders, editor-in-chief Patricia Harty and publisher Niall O'Dowd welcome President Clinton to *Irish America*'s Top 100 Awards, 1996.

(Background, opposite) Actress Maureen O'Hara and publisher Niall O'Dowd, 1995.

THE IMMIGRANT EXPERIENCE AND THE QUEST FOR IDENTITY

Samuel Beckett, an Irishman who chose to emigrate to France rather than America, might well have confronted a survey of the Irish immigrant experience with the question: "But what does it all mean?" and an even more succinct reply, such as "Godot knows."

A somewhat fuller assessment of the subject requires answers to two basic questions rather than one: "What have they done?" and "What will they do?" Or, to put things less cryptically: "What have the Irish accomplished during their three-hundred-year presence in America?' and "Is there still a distinct Irish community in America, with a definable role to play?"

WRESTLING WITH HISTORY

Among the many names that Gaelic bards bestowed upon Ireland, the most evocative was *Inisfail*—Isle of Destiny. More profoundly than the familiar images of the land—green fields, sparkling lakes, mists, and mountains—this mystical idea of a destiny that the Irish carried with them at home or abroad affected countless generations of Gaels. Their destiny was expressed in their history—and this made them a people obsessed with it.

The Irish are forever wrestling with History. Cast down in apparent defeat, they spring up again and renew the struggle, ever conscious of their alter-

Eviction scene, 1888. The Irish have faced persecution in one form or another throughout their history.

nating triumphs and tragedies over the centuries. Haunted by an acute awareness of their tribal experience, the Irish balance optimism with pessimism—the "smile and the tear" of the popular ballad—knowing that it is their destiny, sooner or later, to be challenged to try yet another fall with history.

When the Irish began coming to America in significant numbers, during the 1700s, they brought with them a historical consciousness of ancient glories—preserved in song, poetry, and folklore—and of a civilizing role during the Dark Ages. There was, too, the painful knowledge of conquest, despoliation, and enslavement. Even those who came to America of their own free will, rather than as banished convicts or indentured servants, were merely exchanging subjugation in one English colony for residence in another. But the degraded status of the Irish at home and in America was counterbalanced by the achievements of their brethren in continental Europe, who had wrestled History so successfully as to turn exile into an epic of prestige and power. Psychologically buoyed by the image of the "Wild Geese," and caught up in the revolutionary spirit of the age, the Irish on both sides of the Atlantic rose against English rule during the last decades of the eighteenth century. While the Irish in Ireland lost this latest round in their struggle to fulfill their destiny, their American cousins shared in the victory that created the United States. This new nation would, henceforth, be part of that arena in which the Irish fought out their fate. More than any other corner of the spreading Irish diaspora, it would become an extension of *Inisfail*.

Alas for Irish expectations: If the United States represented an extension of *Inisfail*, it was also very much an extension of *Albion*. The War for Independence had ended English rule, but English attitudes toward the Irish would survive for many generations. In the Anglo-American reading of history, the Irish were a savage, inferior species, treacherous and priest-ridden, given to violence and whisky. To be sure, many of these negative traits had been ascribed to all Americans by their English overlords, and were not unknown to Anglo-American citizens of Jefferson's "Republic of Virtue." But Catholicism was, and would long remain, the distinguishing mark of Irish "otherness." Protestant immigrants from Ireland, such as Confederate General Patrick Cleburne, E.L. Godkin, editor of *The Nation*, William Ford, the father of auto-maker Henry, or the grandfather of Henry and William James—America's leading novelist and psychologist—were accepted readily as full-fledged Americans. Presbyterian Ulstermen

(Left) Outward Bound. Lithograph. Irish immigrant leaving for America.

(Right) Homeward Bound. Lithograph. Prosperous Irish immigrant reviews opportunity to return home.

New Irish immigrants passing through Broadway on a horse-drawn cart as bystanders sneer.

encouraged the use of the term "Scotch-Irish" to make clear to their fellow citizens that they were not "mere Irish."

But the majority of Irish immigrants were Catholics, who could not—or would not—cast off their religious identity. Not all of them were ardent, or even regularly observant, members of the Church. But Catholicism had become an ingrained element of the cultural tradition that the Irish had defended in their long resistance to English domination. It had become an emblem of nationality that some clung to out of defiance as much as out of faith. Their double-labeling as "Irish Catholic" subjected the immigrants in the 1820s and 1830s to both religious discrimination and nativist venom. In the "old country," they had been considered alien, even though legally British subjects. In their new country, their expectation of starting afresh in a land of unbounded opportunity was rudely disappointed. As the stereotypes and suspicions that England had exported to its transatlantic colony confronted them, the immigrants of the early nineteenth century had to wrestle with the History that had been built up over centuries of fear and anger in the British Isles, and try to shape a new History for themselves in America. Their prime tactic during this period was hard work: building the canals and roads of the young nation, patiently enduring the dirty chores and the dirty dwelling places of its cities, and asserting their loyalty to America, even while confronting their fellow Americans' assaults on their religious and fraternal institutions.

In the 1840s, as the Irish Americans were striving to stand upright, to win tolerance and acceptance, History hurled them to the mat through the impact of the Famine. Refugees poured into the United States by the tens and then the hundreds of thousands—diseased, desperate, disoriented. As their numbers swelled, Anglo-Americans found themselves obliged to deal with a new underclass in the cities of the eastern seaboard. The Irish immigrant, previously perceived as a necessary nuisance—a source of cheap labor, despite his Popish superstitions and his cultural eccentricities—now took on a more sinister aspect, that of the beggar, the rioter, the criminal. As a result of the massive Famine era immigration, the Irish in America had to wrestle not only with intensified religious bigotry and nativist political persecution, but with a profound social discrimination that would endure for generations.

During the Civil War and the postwar decades, the Irish fought their way back into the mainstream of American society. They helped to save the Union—and to build labor unions. They moved beyond the East to join the great national enterprise of taming the West. And those who remained in the East laid the foundation for urban, industrial America, while creating the political machine to run its great cities. Permitted now to form a service and administrative infrastructure for an emerging world power, they struggled to rise out of the working class to which most of them were still confined, and some succeeded spectacularly, wrestling their way into the ranks of the nouveau riche. Most continued to strive with minimal reward, too numerous to be marginalized, but still stigmatized as hyphenated Americans.

The struggle against economic discrimination had become the most important issue for those Irish immigrants and their children who still found themselves wrestling with History as the twentieth century dawned.

For others, the stamp of "respectability" was the most important prize of all. The Irish, by the time of the First World War, were furnishing the stars of sport and entertainment, and had become almost honorary Anglo-Saxons through the sheer familiarity of their presence. Yet the American

Augustus Saint Gaudens (1848–1907), Irish-born American sculptor.

elite still undervalued their contributions and denied them full equality. Achievements in the business world were attributed to "Scotch Irish" ancestry; artists and writers of Irish origin were redesignated as "British"—after all, the great architect, Louis Sullivan, had a Belgian mother, and the great sculptor, Augustus St. Gaudens, had a French father. The struggle against snobbery proved the hardest of all. Although the bourgeois gentlemen of the American Irish Historical society, and their ilk, sought to prove that the Irish had ancient and honorable roots in America, their efforts generated little more than dismissive shrugs. As they persisted with their efforts on through the 1920s, documenting the Irish ancestral links of such luminaries as Charles Lindbergh and Calvin Coolidge, they became ever more irrelevant.

During the decades between the close of the "war to end all wars," and the onset of the seemingly endless "Cold War," the Irish won their own war to capture a secure and respected position in America. They had proved their loyalty and their values to their adopted country. Both individually and collectively they had accomplished great things in politics and commerce, high art and popular culture, the mobilization of labor, and the provision of service. Those who had started out Catholic had, despite some defections and a good deal of internal squabbling, persuaded the rest of the population to trust them, even to the point of handing over the keys of the White House and the trigger of the nuclear arsenal. Even if they were not all quite as elegantly assimilated as President Kennedy, they could, by the time of his inauguration, feel that they were truly accepted as Americans. Not all were deemed respectable, but then, some people were never going to be satisfied. No need to go on wrestling with History, they were, finally, at ease in Eden.

"FASHIONABLE TO BE IRISH"

The great accomplishment of the Irish during the three hundred years of their immigration to America had been their turning an often unpromising history into a tale of material and spiritual fulfillment: they seemed poised, like the American Indian, to vanish into the picturesque imagery of the past.

Then came the resurgence of the national question in Ireland, the revival of cultural traditions in America, the explosion of ethnic activism and multicultural enterprise, and the widespread repudiation of the melting pot model. By 1975, as the American Revolution Bicentennial Administration prepared for the country's 200th birthday, the Irish representative took a leading part in the work of its ethnic and racial advisory committee. Endorsing the spirit of the age, he declared that the United States was not a melting pot, but a nation of nations, which ought to acknowledge its ethnic diversity, and celebrate it. This ethnic enthusiasm was, in turn, stimulated by the new wave of "just off the plane" Irish, both documented and undocumented. From the early 1980s onward, so striking was this transition from nearly vanishing to highly visible that the arbiters of social trends declared that it was "fashionable to be Irish."

President Ronald Reagan became one of the millions of Irish descendants who enthusiastically explored their Irish roots during the 1980s.

Children Playing Ball, 1909, **Boston. Photograph by Lewis Hine.**

Presumably it is not merely a desire to be in fashion that led more than twenty million Americans to identify themselves to the census takers as Irish, and more than forty million as partially of Irish ancestry. Awareness of, and pride in, Irish identity had not been so much in evidence only a few decades earlier. President Reagan explained in 1981 that he had grown up without any knowledge of his Irish ancestry, and had never had much occasion—personally or politically—to think about it. Now, he declared, he was finding great satisfaction in tracing his roots.

But did all these born-again Irish constitute an Irish-American community? Geographically, they had spilled out of their erstwhile enclaves, and were found everywhere from the Virgin Islands to the Hawaiian Islands. Occupationally, they might be anything from Washington power brokers to Boston trash-handlers. Politically, they were as likely to be Republicans as Democrats. In terms of their Irish cultural consciousness, they might be versed in the intricacies of Joyce and Yeats and the contemporary insights of Seamus Heaney, fans of Irish pop musicians and Irish-American soccer clubs, or simply parade-goers and "drowners of the shamrock" on March 17th. Not all of them shared an enthusiasm for the nationalist gunmen of Belfast and Londonderry. As a pressure group, they left much to be desired, and as a market for "ethnic items" they were embarrassingly unpredictable. In other words, the usual quantifiable and comfortingly reliable standards of "community" labeling can not be applied here. And yet, there is an undeniable Irishness lingering amidst the ethnic and racial complexities of the American population. Their accents are heard not only in the pub chatter of the latest would-be yuppies from Dublin and Donegal, but in the speech patterns and vocabularies of many regions. Their names are borne not only by the descendants of Irish immigrants, but by those whose ancestors thought that an Irish name sounded more "American" than their own (like Admiral Arleigh Burke, whose grandfather was a Bjorkgren from Sweden). This phenomenon, incidentally, is not limited to surnames: witness the popularity of "Kevin" among blacks, Hispanics, and Asians, and of "Brian" among Jews and Italians.

The Irish-American community at the end of the twentieth century may be amorphous and dispersed, but it is, in an odd way, preserved by its very diffusion. More than any other ethnic group, its historical longevity and its geographical pervasiveness ensure its survival, despite all the forces of assimilation. The St. Patrick's Day cliché, "Everybody's Irish Today," contains a kernel of truth: many people find in Irishness a short cut, as it were, to being American.

Despite the variety of their circumstances and lifestyles, the Irish Americans have a common identity growing out of their unique historical

The Coyne family returns to Minnesota after a trip to Ireland and the Irish relatives, 1930s.

experience, which links them to all of the other groups in the American "nation of nations." Like the Indians, they were robbed of their land. Like the blacks, they were enslaved. Like the Asians, they were subjected to racial caricature and mockery. Like the Jews, they suffered religious persecution. Like the Hispanics, they were derided for clinging to their cultural traditions. Like every other immigrant group, they had to face the hostility and rivalry of those who had arrived earlier and feared the undercutting of their own position.

The Irish immigrant experience is the prototypical immigrant experience, and it may be that in this fact lies the essence of a community that joins together all those millions who claim an Irish-American identity. Theirs is a community of historical adversity and perseverance.

Furthermore, if there remains a distinctive role for this Irish-American community in the twenty-first century, it may well be that of guide and mentor to the latest influx of immigrants, whose way to America—and in America—is often as perilous as that traveled by the Irish. For the American Irish to fully understand their history, learn from it, and pass on its lessons to the strangers who confront similar obstacles today, is no array of easy tasks. Not all of them have absorbed the lessons that past bigotry and racism should have taught them. Indeed, in an odd twist of history, the last arrivals from Ireland are leaving a country in which African and Middle Eastern refugees are now settling. "Ireland for the Irish" signs and race-baiting flyers have appeared in the streets of Dublin. Nevertheless, if the Irish-American community can rise above the prejudices that were directed against their own people in earlier days, if they can share the collective wisdom derived from the Irish experience with the latest arrivals in this nation of immigrants, it will render perhaps the noblest of its countless services to America.

Douglas "Wrong Way" Corrigan, aviator. After announcing he was taking off for California, Corrigan landed in Dublin, Ireland with his $900 Crate, July 18th, 1938, after a flight of 28 hours, 13 minutes from Floyd Bennett Field, New York.

"Douglas Corrigan and His $900 Crate"

A CLOSER LOOK:
THE PRIZE

Winning a Pulitzer Prize is not part of every Irish immigrant's experience.

In 1997, Frank McCourt joined the roster of generals, labor leaders, politicians, and entrepreneurs who have "made it" in their adopted country, when his memoir, *Angela's Ashes*, achieved that distinction. The book tells the story of his family's return to Ireland after a brief, failed stay in Brooklyn. (The Depression was not the ideal time to have migrated to the "Land of Opportunity.") He recounts the vicissitudes and absurdities of growing up in Limerick with a literary skill that has won critics' plaudits, and ends with his second immigration to America, as a young man in the 1950s. His career as an English teacher in New York City schools, and his post-retirement decision to settle down to the business of writing are not the stuff of high drama, like the spectacular doings of a Meagher or the rags-to-riches sagas of the Nevada Silver Kings, but they are close to the norm of the Irish immigrant experience, and the first part of his story has raised great expectations.

(Background) **Frank McCourt at home in Brooklyn, New York.**

(Above) **Ellen Frey, Frank McCourt, and Jeff Gaynor at the tribute to Beckett given by the Irish Repertory Theatre.**

(Left) **The McCourt brothers with their mother, Angela.**

The glorious St. Patrick's stained glass window at Gasson Hall, Boston College.

IRISH GENEALOGY ON THE INTERNET
By Diana Hanson

Before the advent of the internet, tracing genealogy was often difficult. Letters written to distant corners of the country and the world were often delayed, misrouted, and sometimes ignored; checks to record offices, clerks, and professional researchers were sent with the hope that the information they provided was accurate and current. Our most personal quest depended on the indeterminate experience of others.

Today, the internet connects hundreds of thousands—even millions—of people, record offices, professional researchers, and private organizations together on the World Wide Web. We are now able to access the expertise and assistance of experienced genealogists all over the world, as well as first-hand information that has been laboriously entered into web pages. With the aid of "search engines" (such as Yahoo, Alta Vista, Excite, and Lycos), all we need to do is type in our family name and we can find others around the world who share not only our family name but our interest in genealogy. By keying into surname lists (1), one-name studies (2), and list servers (3), even our most distant relatives can be found.

Contacting others with the same surname and interest is the first step in the process of exploring genealogy on the internet. The second step is to organize that information. Here too the web provides a family group sheet (4) and pedigree chart (5) that can be printed out and used to categorize our personal history.

Here are several sources, available right at home, that should be consulted when filling in these forms:

Family Bibles. Ask *every* relative you know for family information.

Family Pictures. Ask relatives to help identify people in the photos; take notice of backgrounds, surroundings, dress style, and dates, and be sure to look on the backs of the pictures.

Family Stories. Most stories, no matter how outrageous, are usually based on some sliver of truth.

Marriage and Death Certificates.

Obituaries and Newspaper Articles.

Family Histories. Check local libraries and genealogical libraries.

Land Records. Families often keep copies of land deeds.

Wills. Families often keep copies of their parents' and grandparents' wills.

The next step is to choose a genealogical line to focus on—too broad a base of information can be confusing. Since we are discussing Irish genealogy, we are going to concentrate on Irish lines, using my own Feeney ancestry from Ireland who came to Dubuque, Iowa, during the potato famine, as an example. The same research methods can be applied to any line during any period of emigration.

The most difficult part of tracing Irish genealogy is locating your ancestral parish (a civil or church designation). Parish registers will contain not only records of births, baptisms, marriages, and deaths, but land and probate records as well.

There are 2508 civil parishes in Ireland. They were originally ecclesiastical divisions that became important civil divisions in their own right, and they often bridge both county and barony boundaries. A townland is the smallest administrative division in Ireland; there are 60,462 townlands in Ireland, and on average each covers about 350 acres. Many townlands share the same name—for example, there are 56 Kilmores and 47 Dromores. A full list is online at the Valuation Office web site (6).

A particularly valuable resource at this point in your search is *General Alphabetical Index to the Townlands and Towns, Parishes, and Baronies of Ireland*, a book that indexes and locates the names of townlands within each parish in all of the counties of Ireland. Based on the 1851 Ireland census, it names more than 60,000 townlands—some extant—and is available in most libraries.

Once you have located the townland within a parish and county, look in the Ireland National Archives (7) for available records.

If you don't already know the name of your ancestors' townland or parish, learn everything you can about your immigrant ancestors in the United States by searching these records:

U.S. Immigration Records (8). If you know the name of the ship your ancestors emigrated on, the *emigration-ship@rootsweb.com* (9) list server can help locate its point of origin and route to America.

U.S. Naturalization Records (available in each county). Start at the US Gen Web site (10) and locate the county where your ancestors lived approximately five to ten, perhaps twenty, years after emigrating. Naturalization was also accomplished by serving in the military during the Civil War, so if they were Irish Famine immigrants between 1840 and 1850 be sure to check the courthouse of the county where they lived during this time.

Marriage and Death Records often give the place of birth (11).

Tombstone Engravings (12).

Census Records (13).

Church Records of marriages or burials, and membership records.

Children's or Sibling Records.

Military Records (14).

Family Histories are available through public libraries and local genealogical societies as well as online by ancestry (15).

Land Records (16).

The above records are easily located through online projects such the US Gen Web Project (17), one of the most extensive genealogical projects in the world. Every county in every state of the United States is represented on the internet. Volunteers, who are often professional and experienced genealogists, maintain web pages describing available records, addresses, resources, and lookups (people who will look up information) for these counties (18). Within days you can have information that used to take months to locate, and at very little cost. There are even online courses (19, 20) that are free of charge to assist you in the process.

Once you've exhausted every possible resource in the United States, it's time to start searching records in Ireland.

Now you can turn to online projects such as the GENUKI (21), the IRLGEN (22), PRONI (Public Record Office of Northern Ireland) (23), TIARA (The Irish Ancestral Research Association) (24), and the World Gen Web Project (25). Hopefully, you will have located the name of your townland and parish in Ireland and will be able to determine what records are available for that county. The tombstone of my immigrant ancestor (John Feeney, b. 1835), who was buried in Garryowen Cemetery, Dubuque County, Iowa, included the name of his parish in Ireland—Dysart in Roscommon County. By searching the online data base I have discovered that Dysart is indeed the name of a parish in Roscommon, its records filed under the letters B and C for that jurisdiction at the National Archives in Dublin (26). These indexes often seem confusing, but it is best to write down *all* the information you find, including designators, for future reference.

It is important to remember when tracing Irish genealogy that all sorts of sociological and historical factors impacted your family

and the records that were kept. Consider such major events as the Irish potato famine of the 1840s and 1850s, the Irish Rebellion of 1798, and the English occupation. A quick study of Irish history (27) shows that there was a time in Ireland when Catholic priests were forbidden to keep records and virtually went "underground" due to English influence and fear of punishment. However, many secret and alternative records such as "parish chests" (a hodge-podge collection of documents) were kept and are slowly coming to light.

Now locate all records that are available for your family's parish (Dysart, in our example) by locating the web page for its county (Roscommon) through a search engine such as Yahoo or Lycos. This will quickly give you the url (address) of the World Gen Web Page (28) listing the addresses of all the parishes and records for (Roscommon) county and similar GENUKI pages (29).

I found maps of Roscommon at several places, again through the search engines (30, 31, 32). The parish of Dysart borders on the county of Galway, and in such a case you may need to search the adjoining parishes for information since families often traveled from one parish to another.

There are national records beginning in 1845 for non-Catholic marriages and civil registrations of births, marriages, and deaths (from 1864) available through the Public Record Office in Dublin. However, before 1864 you must search the local church records for births, baptisms, marriages, and deaths. The county pages for Roscommon, for instance, show that although there are no Catholic Church Records for Dysart before 1850, the parish of Cam to the northeast has records to 1835. Taghboy, to the north, is included in the parish registers of Dysart, and Taghmaconnel to the south has records to 1842. So if your ancestors were born before this time, you may have difficulty locating the family, but there is still hope.

Many genealogists try to fill in every date for every person on their family groups sheets and often overlook other documents recording civil, legal, or family connections that will provide important information. Before 1850 it might be hard to find exact dates but you will be probably be able to locate family groups through records such as the following (available in Roscommon County and, in similar form, in every county in Ireland):

1911 Census (33).

1901 Census Dublin (33).

1894 *Slater's Royal National Directory of Ireland* lists traders, police, teachers, farmers, and private residents in each of the towns, villages, and parishes of the county.

1881 *Slater's Royal National Commercial Directory of Ireland.*

1870 *Slater's Directory of Ireland.*

1856 *Slater's Royal National Commercial Directory of Ireland.*

1847–48 *Tenants from Ballykilcline Who Emigrated Under State-Aided Scheme.*

1846 *Slater's National Commercial Directory of Ireland.*

1836–44 List of Qualified Voters is arranged alphabetically giving addresses.

1824 *J. Pigot's City of Dublin & Hibernian Provincial Directory* includes some County Roscommon information.

1823–38 Tithe Applotment Survey (34).

1813–21 List of Freeholders (NLI ILB 324).

1780 List of Freeholders (LDS Film #100181) (35).

1749 Religious Census of Elphin Diocese (35).

1661 Indexes to Marriage Licenses back to 1661.

1659 Census of Ireland (35).

1650 Wills and Administrations back to 1650.

Many people who study history know that Four Courts, the national repository for the records of Ireland, burned to the ground in 1855, leaving only one wing standing. While many records were destroyed, as you can see from the list above (relating only to Roscommon county, of course), there are many substitute records for the missing census and parish registers. And there are similar lists for every county in Ireland.

If you can't locate the films or books yourself, there are professional researchers (36) who can be hired to do the research for you. And don't assume you will save money by doing it yourself; you may well spend as much, or more, asking the National Archives to do one small search at a time.

There are also many family histories available on the County pages that have appeared in newspapers printed since 1828; residents who emigrated to the U.S. are very likely to be named. The GENUKI (Genealogy for the United Kingdom and Ireland) (21) and the World Gen Web Pages (37) also give miscellaneous records and research services and societies that are available to help you. All of this information can be found by searching the internet. You have only to push that first button!

LINK REFERENCES:

1   *http://www.usgenweb.com/links/surname.htm/*

2   *http://www.leicester.co.uk/guild/*

3   *http://www.usgenweb.com/links/newsgroupslinks.htm*

4   *http://www.ideaschool.org/courses/general/famgrp.htm*

5   *http://www.ideaschool.org/courses/general/pedigree.htm*

6   *http://www.campus.bt.com/CampusWorld/pub/OS/Gazetteer/index.html*

7   *http://www.kst.dit.ie/nat-arch/genealogy.html*

8   *http://www.history.rochester.edu/jssn/page2.htm*

9   *emigration-ship@rootsweb.com* (e-mail address)

10 *http://www.usgenweb.com/*

11 *http://www.ideaschool.org/courses/general/gen110_5.htm*

12 *http://www.ideaschool.org/courses/general/gen110_9.htm*

13 *http://www.ideaschool.org/courses/general/gen110_6.htm*

14 *http://www.history.rochester.edu/jssn/page5.htm*

15 *http://www.ideaschool.org/courses/general/gen110_4.htm*

16 *http://www.ultranet.com/~deeds/landref.htm*

17 *http://www.usgenweb.com/*

18 *http://www.rootsweb.com/~iaduduqu/index.html*

19 *http://www.ideaschool.org/courses/general/gen208.htm*

20 *http://csc.techcenter.org*

21 *http://midas.ac.uk/genuki/big/*

22 *http://www.bess.tcd.ie/irlgen/genweb2.htm*

23 *http://proni.nics.gov.uk/index.htm,*

24 *http://world.std.com/~ahern/TIARA.html*

25 *http://www.geocities.com/Athens/Parthenon/5341/index.html*

26 *http://www.kst.dit.ie/nat-arch/genealogy.html*

27 *http://www.ideaschool.org/courses/general/gen208_2.htm*

28 *http://www.geocities.com/5341/roscommon.htm*

29 *http://www.bess.tcd.ie/irlgen/Roscomm.htm.*

30 *http://www.thecore.com/let_ros/ros_bar.html,*

31 *http://www.thecore.com/let_ros/ros_rcpar.html*

32 *http://www.bess.tcd.ie/irlen/connmap.htm*

33 *http://www.kst.dit.ie/nat-arch/genealogy.html.*

34 *http://www.bess.tcd.ie/irlgen/tithe.htm*

35 *http://www.interdys.org/ to locate the nearest LDS Family History Center*

36 *http://www.bess.tcd.ie/irlgen/heritage.htm*

37 *http://www.geocities.com/Athens/Parthenon/5341/index.html*

THE 50 BEST IRELAND URLS TO KNOW ON THE INTERNET!

MISCELLANEOUS:

1. Facts About Ireland - Culture -
   http://www.irlgov.ie/iveagh/foreignaffairs/facts/fai/CHAPTER7/HOME7.html
This source provides information, divided into categories, about the local culture in areas such as literature, drama, art, music, cinema, folklore, architecture, etc.

2. Proto-Heraldry in Early Christian Ireland -
   http://www.finearts.sfasu.edu/uasal/irherald.html
A great explanation of the battle arms of Irish chieftains—a rare find! This is a well-documented source that will lead you to other information on the internet concerning Irish clans, chieftains, and heraldry.

3. Scottish and Irish Clan Designations -
   http://www.lubbock.com/mclaurin/
A dealer of books and genealogical information, and one of the best sources for finding Irish clan and name explanations currently on the internet. A fee is required for this source.

4. Heraldry in Ireland -
   http://www.finearts.sfasu.edu/uasal/heraldry.html
A good explanation of the proto-heraldry that was common in Ireland for those interested in coats of arms.

5. Fred Hanna's Bookstore - Dublin - *http://www.hannas.ie/*
A treasure chest of books concerning Ireland, Irish history, and genealogy. This is the place to find old books concerning lost records of parishes and census returns that were thought to have been destroyed.

6. Kenny's Books On-line -
   http://www.iol.ie/resource/kennys/books.html
Another great source for finding those lost treasures, rare books, antiquities, and information about the people and the area you are researching. You can order this source directly over the internet.

7. British and Irish Authors -
   http://lang.nagoya-u.ac.jp/index-e.html
How better to understand the people of Ireland than through their writings and poetry? Hidden insights into local happenings are often found in the poetic writings of the local bards—or perhaps your relation was an author himself!

8. Dublin, Ireland, Unofficial Home Page -
   http://ireland.iol.ie/~dco/
This unofficial home page of Dublin often gives insight into local happenings, cultural events, and displays featuring the history of Ireland, and can uncover new leads to pursue in your search.

HISTORY:

9. Irish History Page -
   http://wwwvms.utexas.edu/~jdana/irehist.html
This is a good place to start for a general understanding of the history of Ireland and how it affected the people and the political structure.

10. History Ireland - *http://www.ucc.ie/histire/*
A great source of historical information about every county of the realm that can help you to understand the immigration and migration patterns of the Irish as well as the feuding between clans and societies.

11. Rebellion Home Page -
   http://www.rtc-carlow.ie/united/98Home.html
An informative look at the 1798 Rebellion—its battles and its effect on local regions—and the people who left Ireland due to political differences.

12. The Potato Famine in History -
   http://www.pilot.infi.net/~cksmith/famine/History.html
The single most profound event that led to Irish emigration was the potato famine, which devastated the food crop of Ireland and caused almost one-third of the population to die of starvation and disease. Another one-third came to other English-speaking countries such as Australia, England, Canada, and the United States. Many fled the dying country with the help of landlords and government agencies. This site gives excellent references for information on the potato famine and how it affected each county.

13. The Irish Famine - 1845–50 -
   http://avery.med.virginia.edu/~eas5e/Irish/Famine.html
This site gives added insight and information concerning the cause and effects of the Famine on the people of Ireland as well as the countries who received their emigrants.

14. Liberation of Ireland - *http://www.iol.ie/~dluby/history.htm*
An in-depth look at the ongoing political battle between the Irish and the English and its effect on Northern Ireland and the religion of the Irish people.

ARCHIVES AND REPOSITORIES:

15. Trinity College - Dublin - *http://www.tcd.ie/*
Trinity College, the oldest university in the world, has the largest collection of rare books and antiquities relating to the history, genealogy, and origin of the people of Ireland. Some of these books date back to the 1300s, the glorious Book of Kells to A.D. 800. It was at Trinity College that the IRLGEN Family History Project was started and continues to grow. Trinity College is also the legal repository of government documents for Ireland and is available for public research.

16. List of Local Heritage Centers -
http://www.bess.tcd.ie/irlgen/heritage.htm
This list of local county heritage centers gives addresses, fees, and contact information for professional researchers in Ireland who can carry out genealogical searches in the local archives.

17. Irish National Archives - *http://www.kst.dit.ie/nat-arch/*
The National Archives located in Dublin is the repository for all known genealogical and historical documents of Ireland including censuses, probates, parish registers, tithe applotment records, immigration and emigration records, and miscellaneous records, all of which are indexed and available for searching. Some, such as the Transportation of Convicts to Australia, are available for online searching.

18. Public Record Office Northern Ireland -
http://proni.nics.gov.uk/
Here is the repository for all genealogical and historical documents relating to Northern Ireland upon its separation from the Republic of Ireland as well as all such documents pertaining to Northern Ireland as far back as the 1600s, some as far back as 1300. A web search agent can search this source for records relating to government, courts of law, and documents deposited by individuals and institutions.

19. Marsh's Library - *http://www.kst.dit.ie/marsh/library.html*
The first public library in Ireland, Marsh's Library has nearly 25,000 books relating to genealogy and the history of Ireland in the 1600s and 1700s and is open to the public for research. Containing the private library of the Bishop of Worcester (1635–99), this source holds hidden treasures that cannot be found anywhere else in the world.

20. Russell Library - *http://www.may.ie/library/file_10.htm*
An excellent source of local and national history and cultural materials, Russell Library has a massive collection of rare and older books, manuscripts, and archives. The oldest books date back to 1460 and contain examples of early writing and early printing methods as well as valuable information about the Irish and Ireland.

21. UCC Library - Cork -
http://booleweb.ucc.ie/special-collections.html
The UCC Library houses an extensive collection of rare and privately printed books relative to Cork before 1800 and also contains historical documents pertaining to historical studies of the 19th century.

22. University College - Galway -
http://sulacco.library.ucg.ie:80/services/info/resources/specialcol.html
University College contains the rare collection of books from Queens College, Galway, dating back to 1800, as well as historical information on Galway County and residents within the county. Also available are Galway's Civic Records or The Corporation Manuscripts, 1485–1818, 1836–1922; the Eyre Deeds, a collection of legal records relating to Galway, 1720–1857; and the Hyde Mss Collection, containing volumes of prose, poetry, and various tracts penned by 18th-century scribes and including miscellaneous manuscripts of Douglas Hyde.

23. Useful Addresses - *http://www.bess.tcd.ie/irlgen/reposit.htm*
With this list of addresses for locating county and regional libraries and repositories, you can now write directly to the source for information to locate books or documents regarding specific topics.

GENEALOGY LINKS:

24. Irish Genealogy Links - John Grenham -
http://indigo.ie/~rfinder/
Maintained by one of Ireland's leading resident genealogists and experts on Dublin genealogy, this site offers links to genealogical resources within Ireland which are useful and categorized, as well as online archives available for searching.

25. Irish Emigrants -
http://genealogy.org/~ajmorris/ireland/ireemg.htm
This list of Irish ships and emigrants arriving in the U.S., Canada, and England is an excellent—although limited—source for genealogists, and should not be ignored since it is constantly growing due to volunteer contributions.

26. Irish Family History Foundation –
    http://www.mayo-ireland.ie/Roots.htm
A full-service genealogical foundation, this page not only offers resources and addresses, but also paid research services, making it easier to cover all the documents available. It also contains links to each local historical and research center for every county.

27. Essential Genealogy Links Page – Sponsored by the House
    of Waterford – *http://www.browseireland.com/geneology/*
A growing and rarely indexed page by the internet web robots, this is an excellent source of Irish genealogy links which may well be missing elsewhere. Maintained by the House of Waterford in Waterford, Ireland, it is more extensive than many others and includes links to home pages about Irish surnames and pedigrees.

28. Irish Genealogical Society International –
    http://mtn.org/mgs/branches/irish.html
This page links Minnesota, home to many Irish immigrants, and Ireland.

29. Irish Surname List –
    http://genealogy.org/~ajmorris/ireland/iresurn.htm
Although not very extensive, this list is one of the few places on the internet that has good information on particular Irish surnames.

30. Ulster Historical Foundation –
    http://www.uhf.org.uk/frames30.htm
Started in 1957 and constantly updated, this source aids in historical and genealogical research in Ulster, Northern Ireland, and although still under construction, promises to be the ultimate resource for Northern Ireland sources, offering an online search as well as yearly conferences.

31. Irish Surname Lists –
    http://www.cs.ncl.ac.uk/genuki/SurnamesList/
Surname lists maintained by the county hosts are available for public posting and often lead you to others who are researching the same lines and with whom you can share information. Invaluable to the inexperienced researcher, they give you links, networking ability, and leads to information concerning your own family.

32. World Gen Web Project Ireland Genealogy Page –
    http://www.geocities.com/Athens/Parthenon/5341/index.html
Recently begun, the World Gen Web Ireland Page is fast becoming *the* source for Irish researchers, maintaining query pages, surname lists, and resource lists for every county in Ireland. The Ireland Gen Web Project is slowly adding to its archives records, including family histories, that have been carried to other countries and are no longer available in Ireland.

33. GENUKI Pages – *http://midas.ac.uk/genuki/mindex.html*
The offical and most complete source for British genealogical research, the GENUKI pages organize information by county within the different countries. They also list surname lists, list servers, and local repositories for every county, making it easier to concentrate on one area at a time.

34. 3rd Irish Genealogical Congress –
    http://www.genealogy.org/~igc/
An international event for genealogists interested in Irish research, the 3rd Irish Genealogical Congress will keep you up to date on the most recent developments in Irish genealogy.

35. IRLGEN Family History Project –
    http://www.bess.tcd.ie/roots_ie.htm
The IRLGEN Project, developed at Trinity College in Dublin, organizes and archives materials relating to family history and genealogical research in Ireland. A great place to look for resources, research methods, and links, this is the place to start when doing Irish genealogical research.

36. Genealogical Guide to Ireland –
    http://www.bess.tcd.ie/irlgen/genweb2.htm
Part of the IRLGEN Project, this is an index to the list of resources, complete with a "get started guide" for the beginning genealogist as well as useful links in locating additional material.

37. Index to Irish Genealogy Guide –
    http://www.bess.tcd.ie/irlgen/links.htm
Part of the IRLGEN Project, this alphabetical index to the genealogical guide helps beginning researchers to locate records faster and more efficiently.

38. Sources (by era) – *http://www.bess.tcd.ie/irlgen/sera.htm*
Separated by era, this index maintained by IRLGEN directs you to specific records for each time period. It names various substitutes for lost census and parish registers, and as such is an invaluable source for locating replacement records.

39. A–Z of British Genealogical Research –
    http://midas.ac.uk/genuki/big/EmeryPaper.html
An alphabetical dictionary and explanation of genealogical terms,

this guide helps you to understand which records are worth searching and how to utilize them. It covers everything from abbreviations to heraldry to handwriting, and even includes a wish list of resources we would like to have available for British genealogical research. Absolutely invaluable!

40. Directory of Royal Genealogy –
   http://www.dcs.hull.ac.uk/public/genealogy/royal/
This directory is essential for those with royal connections. It not only lists the royal families of England and Great Britain, but also the kings of Ireland and all the other royal families of Europe, including Jerusalem and the Islamic Dynasties.

41. Old and New Style Dates –
   http://midas.ac.uk/genuki/big/dates.txt
Because the Gregorian calendar was not adopted in England until 1752, many dates of birth, marriage, and death are ambiguous and hard to interpret. This treatise on old and new style dates and the different calendars that were used can help clarify how the calendar affects genealogical research.

42. Genealogy Before the Parish Registers –
   ftp://sable.ox.ac.uk/pub/users/malcolm/genealogy/pro/rio28.txt
After you have exhausted the most widely used documents such as parish registers and civil registrations, this is a good source for the availability of records before parish registers and provides some strategies involved in doing genealogical research.

43. Military Records –
   http://chide.museum.org.uk/military.index.html
For those with ancestors who served in the British military this is an excellent resource for locating histories of different colonial regiments and military elements. It is also linked to other resources for locating military records throughout the British Empire.

44. Irish Genealogy Page –
   http://wwwvms.utexas.edu/~jdana/history/genealogy.html
This site, maintained by a University of Texas student, is a good place to start Irish research. Updated frequently, it contains new sources of information.

MAPS:
45. Interactive Maps of Ireland –
   http://starti.ucd.ie/maps/ireland.html
A good source for finding current locations on general maps of Ireland, you can click your way from county to county for boundaries and major thoroughfares.

NEWSGROUPS AND LIST SERVERS:
46. *news.soc.genealogy.uk+ireland* –
A great list server for finding out information about the availability of records and for sharing information with others.

47. *news.clari.world.europe.ireland* –
Another good list server for finding out sources of information and sharing information with others.

48. *emigration-ships-L@rootsweb.com* - (e-mail address)
An excellent list server for finding out information about specific ships, passengers, and ports of entry. The members are very knowledgeable and thorough and are willing to share information. Be aware when you subscribe that their mailings are very heavy!

CLASSES FOR IRISH GENEALOGY:
49. Ideaschool Free Ireland Genealogy Class –
   http://www.ideaschool.org/courses/general/gen208.htm
An excellent class, free of charge, that takes you from the beginning steps of organizing your research to locating and hopefully searching the records needed to complete your Irish genealogy to the best of your ability. Taught by an accredited genealogist, this is the perfect class for the beginning as well as the more advanced student of genealogy.

50. Carl Sandburg College Internet Genealogy Class –
   http://csc.techcenter.org/~mneill/csc.html
An excellent course in exploring genealogy over the internet, this is a fairly inexpensive class that offers online instruction covering the basic sources and research methods.

INDEX

Page numbers in *italics* indicate illustrations.

PHOTO CREDITS

Cover illustration: Minnesota Historical Society; pp. 10–11, 12: Christopher Hill Photographic; p. 14: Kit DeFever; p. 15: National Museum of Ireland; p. 16: National Gallery of Ireland; p. 17: Irish Tourist Board, Dublin; pp. 18–19: Irish Tourist Board; p. 20: National Museum of Ireland; p. 21: Trinity College, Dublin; pp. 22–3: Brown University Military Collection; p. 24: University College, Dublin; p. 26: Trinity College, Dublin; p. 27: National Library of Ireland; p. 28: National Library of Ireland; p. 29: Missouri Historical Society, St. Louis; p. 30: Corbis-Bettmann; p. 31: Library of Congress; p. 33: Library of Congress; pp. 34–5: University College, Dublin; p. 36: Cameo Photography, Loughrea; p. 38: Brown Brothers; p. 39: *Portland Press Herald*, Portland, ME; p. 40: Courtesy, American Antiquarian Society; p. 41: Library of Congress; p. 42: Archive Photos; p. 43: Archive Photos; p. 44: Courtesy, American Antiquarian Society; p. 45 (left): Archive Photos; p. 45 (right): Brown Brothers; p. 46: Courtesy, American Antiquarian Society; p. 47: Courtesy, American Antiquarian Society/Artist: John Neagle, 1835; p. 48: Archive Photos; p. 49: University College, Dublin; p. 51 (background): Archive Photos; pp. 52–3: University College, Dublin; p. 54: Museum of the City of New York; p. 56: National Library of Ireland; p. 57: National Library of Ireland; p. 58: Corbis-Bettman; p. 59: Library of Congress; p. 60: The Metropolitan Museum of Art; p. 61: Archive Photos; pp. 62–3: Museum of the City of New York; p. 64: Courtesy, American Antiquarian Society; p. 65: Archive Photos; p. 66: Library of Congress; p. 67 (top): Courtesy, American Antiquarian Society; p. 67 (bottom): Library of Congress; p. 68: Library of Congress; p. 69: Courtesy, American

Antiquarian Society; p. 70: Corbis-Bettman; p. 71: Museum of the City of New York; pp. 72–3: Bettmann Archives; pp. 74–5: Museum of the City of New York; p. 76: National Portrait Gallery; p. 78: Library of Congress; p. 79: Library of Congress: pp. 80–81: Courtesy, Don Troiani, Southbury, CT; p. 82 (left and below): Courtesy, Ron Tunison; p. 83: Archive Photos; p. 84: Library of Congress; p. 85: Library of Congress; pp. 86–7: Archive Photos; p. 88: Brown Brothers; p. 89: Library of Congress; p. 91: Courtesy, American Antiquarian Society; p. 92 (top): Courtesy, American Antiquarian Society; p. 92 (lbottom): Courtesy, American Antiquarian Society; p. 93 (above): Corbis-Bettmann; p. 93 (below): Archive Photos/American Stock; p. 94: B.F. Childs, The Minnesota Historical Society; p. 95 (above): Bettmann Archives; p. 95 (right): Corbis-Bettmann; p. 97: Museum of the City of New York; p. 99: Courtesy, American Antiquarian Society; p. 100: Statue of Liberty/Ellis Island; p. 101 (above): Brown Brothers; p. 101 (right): Brown Brothers; p. 102: Brown Brothers; p. 103: Museum of the City of New York; p. 104: Courtesy, American Antiquarian Society; p. 105: George S. Harris & Sons, Museum of the City of New York, Gift of William G. Schmidt; p. 106: Corbis-Bettmann; p. 107: Library of Congress; p. 108: Boston College Audio Visual; p. 109: Courtesy *The World of Hibernia* Magazine; pp. 108–109: Text edited with permission of Thomas J. O'Gorman from his article in *The World of Hibernia* Magazine; p. 110 (above): Courtesy, Union Pacific Railroad Museum; p. 110 (left): Union Pacific Museum Collection; p. 111: Union Pacific Museum Collection/Andrew J. Russell; p. 112: Library of Congress; p. 113: Institute of Texan Cultures; p. 114 (top): Institute of Texan Cultures; p. 114 (left): Institute of Texan Cultures; p. 115: Institute of Texan Cultures; p. 116: Brown Brothers; p. 117: Brown Brothers; pp. 118–19: Museum of the City of New

York; p. 120: Hirz/Archive Photos; p. 122: Collection of Eileen McCormick Lawton; p. 123 (top): The Statue of Liberty National Monument at Ellis Island; p. 123 (bottom): Brown Brothers; p. 124: Brown Brothers; p. 125: Brown Brothers; p. 126: Library of Congress; p. 127: Library of Congress; p. 128: Brown Brothers; p. 129: Private Collection; p. 130: Library of Congress; p. 131: Archive Photos; p. 133: Archive Photos/Blank Archives; p. 134: Library of Congress; p. 135 (top): Colorado Historical Society; p. 135 (bottom): Brown Brothers; p. 136: Brown Brothers; p. 137: Museum of the City of New York; p. 138: Brown Brothers; p. 139: Archive Photos; p. 141: Detroit Institute of Arts; p. 142: Collection of Eileen McCormick Lawton; p. 143: Jacob Riis; p. 145: Hirz/Archive Photos; p. 146: Library of Congress; p. 147: Library of Congress; p. 148: The Society for the Preservation of New England Antiquities; p. 149: Brown Brothers; p. 150: Brown Brothers; p. 151: Detroit Institute of Arts; p. 152: Staten Island Historical Society; p. 153: Brown Brothers; p. 154: Minnesota Historical Society/Montgomery Christman; p. 155: Minnesota Historical Society; pp. 156–7: Archive Photos; p. 158: Brown Brothers; p. 160: Archive Photos/fotos International; p. 161: Brown Brothers; p. 162: Brown Brothers; p. 163: UPI/Corbis-Bettmann; p. 164: UPI/Corbis-Bettmann; p. 165: Archive Photos; p. 166: Library of Congress; p. 167: Archive Photos; p. 168: Archive Photos/Museum of the City of New York; p. 169: Hirz/Archive Photos; p. 171: Brown Brothers; p. 172: Archive Photos; p. 173: AP/Wirephoto; p. 174: Beaver Island Historical Society; p. 174: Text edited with permission of Beaver Island Historical Society and Helen Collar: p. 175: Library of Congress: p. 176: Archive Photos/fotos International; p. 177: Archive Photos; p. 178: Archive Photos; p. 179: Archive Photos; p. 180: Archive Photos/Columbia Pictures; p. 181 (above): Archive Photos; p. 181 (right): Archive

Photos; p. 182 (top): Archive/American Stock: p. 182 (bottom): Archive Photos: pp. 182–3 (background): Archive Photos: p. 183: Archive Photos; p. 184 (above): Archive Photos; p. 184 (left): Archive Photos/UPI; p. 185: Archive Photos; p. 186: Archive Photos; p. 187: Archive Photos/20th Century-Fox; pp. 188–9: Collection of Dr. and Mrs. Quentin Murphy; p. 190: Archive Photos/fotos International; p. 192: UPI/Corbis-Bettmann; p. 193: Corbis-Bettmann; p. 195: Archive Photos; p. 197: Oistin MacBride/Corbis-Bettman; p. 198:

Archive Photos/Reuters/Jonathan Hession; p. 199: Archive Photos/Reuters/Stringer; p. 200: Collection of William D. Griffin; p. 202: Archive Photos/Reuters/Peter Morgan; p. 205: Archive Photos/Ricardo Watson; p. 206: Archive Photos/Reuters/Ray Stubblebine; p. 207: Archive Photos/Reuters/Stephen Jaffe; p. 209: Archive Photos; p. 210 & 211: Courtesy *Irish America* Magazine: pp. 212–13: Christopher Hill Photographic: p. 214: Archive Photos/Reuters/Peter Morgan; p. 216: National Library of Ireland; p. 217

(left): Corbis-Bettman; p. 217 (right): Corbis-Bettmann; p. 218: Bettmann Archives; p. 220: Archive Photos/Museum of the City of New York; p. 221: Archive Photos; p. 222: Lewis W. Hine/Courtesy George Eastman House, Rochester, NY; p. 224: Minnesota Historical Society; p. 225: Archive Photos; p. 226 (background and left): Courtesy *Irish America* Magazine; p. 226 (above): James Higgins; p. 227: Courtesy Department of Publications and Print Marketing, Boston College/Gary Gilbert; Endsheets: Courtesy American Antiquarian Society; Back cover illustration: AP/Wide World Photos.